To my beautiful family for their love and support.

Diary of a Pregnant Grandfather

Wayne Anderson

Table of Contents

Chapter 1

A Speeding Truck

I was a wreck. I felt like I'd just been run over by a fully loaded tractor-trailer careening down the highway. It was mid-August, late at night, and I was lying in bed staring at the ceiling in the dark, not able to sleep.

I'm tough. I have faced very tough situations while in the Marine Corps, and also as a business executive, and I always prided myself that I am able to take the emotion out of situations so I can look at them calmly and rationally. But not this one. I'm up against something that I've never faced before.

My daughter and son-in-law casually told my wife and I earlier this evening that they are having a baby, which translates into "*I'm going to be grandfather.*" Those words kept racing around and around in my mind.

They were pretty sneaky about it too. They came to visit us for the weekend. Not unusual. We live approximately four hours apart, basically from one end of Pennsylvania to the other. Usually we get to see them only at holidays, or during my vacation when we make the trek to their house.

As I looked at it, I guess you could say that it's payback time for me. After dragging my family around the United States for eleven years while I was in the service, my wife, daughter, son, and I finally settled in south central Pennsylvania "to put down some roots." We managed to stay in the same place for fourteen years (something they had never known) which is where the kids grew up, made friends, and graduated from high school.

Looking back on it, I should have seen that a perfect storm was brewing, but I missed it completely. We had a lot of things going on at the time which led to where we are now.

It so happened at that time that our daughter had just graduated from college and moved back in with us while she searched for her first job. Our son had moved out and was attending a two year technical school in Pittsburgh. Maybe he saw the storm coming that I didn't. It was also at that same time that I had been interviewing for a job that I really wanted, and just gotten the answer that I was looking for...I was hired. The bad part of the whole thing was that the job was in Kansas City, nine hundred miles from where we lived. This meant that we were folding up the tent and heading to the Midwest.

I should probably insert here that I had always told the kids (kidding, of course) that when they had both graduated from high school, their mother and I were moving and not leaving any forwarding address. Boy, did that come back to haunt me.

I gathered the two women in my family into the kitchen, and proceeded to tell my daughter of my good fortune, and that she was going to have to make other living arrangements because we were moving to Kansas City. It was at that point our kitchen became ground zero for a nuclear blast.

"You're moving? What about me? Where am I going to live? Are you just throwing me out? Will I get your new address, or are you moving in the middle of the night?"

Oh boy, this didn't work out the way I had planned.

After several nights in a row of rehashing the situation, we were able to work our way through it. Luckily my daughter got a job, and found a very nice apartment owned by one of the ladies at her work. It was just a one bedroom apartment in a building in the historical section of town. After a few anxious nights in the beginning, she found that living alone wasn't all that bad. She really grew up during that time and became independent. As much consternation and anxious moments that it created, it was one of the better decisions that we made.

Back to the big announcement.

My daughter and son-in-law arrived at the house late on Friday night. They had both worked most of the day, and had left in the late afternoon. We were all in the living room relaxing and talking about the trip and other various things, when my daughter got up from the couch and said she had something for us.

She went over by the front door and picked up a small plastic grocery bag and came back into the room. She pulled out a long paper-wrapped object and gave it to my wife. She opened it and found that it was a spoon and knife we had left at their house on the last visit. She then pulled out a bigger object from the bag and handed it to my wife. I couldn't see what it was at that point.

It's important that you understand at this point where everyone was seated. My wife and daughter were on the sofa in front of the large windows in the living room, my son-in-law was seated on the adjacent wall sitting in an overstuffed chair, and I was on the other side of the small table with a light on it that was between he and I. I was in "Dad's chair", my favorite recliner facing the TV. Good thing.

My wife pulled the object out of the bag and looked at it for a moment. Nothing registered on her face. Ok, nothing important.

Then her face sort of melted and she began crying and breathing hard. She also started doing this thing that was sort of like running in place. I had only seen her do this one time before. We had been married for only a short time, and I startled her one time when I walked into the bathroom while she was fixing her hair, and she did the same thing. Ran in place. I laughed and asked where she was going, but I got a response that I thought was totally inappropriate from a woman who was my wife.

So there's my wife, running in place, crying and clutching this object, and hugging my daughter. I'm across the room, sitting in my chair, going "What? What? What is it?"

My wife has now moved onto our son-in-law and is hugging him. My daughter turns and looks at me, "I'm pregnant."

Wham! There goes that speeding tractor-trailer.

It was at that moment I realized we had all just made a huge transition in an instant, but it was mostly my daughter. She didn't look any different, she didn't act any different, at least within the first thirty minutes of the visit. It was at this very point that a video of scenes started flashing through my mind...

The day she was born and my wife making fun of me as I held our small daughter and explained Einstein's theory of relativity to her. I still think it's the reason she's so smart.

Me tossing a small, red ball to her while she held a Flintstone-sized plastic bat.

Holding her hand before she got her wisdom teeth out.

Meeting her and my wife at the hospital emergency room when she got hit in the face by a softball while playing second base during a game.

Teaching her to drive, and getting into an argument, and then laughing about it afterwards.

Watching her cross the stage as she graduated from college,

and embarrassing her as I stood and whaooed.

Nervously walking her down the aisle on her wedding day hoping I didn't trip.

Now, she had made the complete transition, like my wife and the millions of women before her, from someone's daughter to someone's (soon-to-be) mother. She had selected her life mate and was starting the next generation of our family.

My wife rolls over and asks me sleepily why I'm still awake. I tell her that it must have been the sugar from the big bowl of ice cream I ate before I went to bed that's keeping me awake. Yeah, that must be it.

Boy, it's going to be a long nine months.

*   *   *

Our daughter swore us to secrecy...we are not allowed to tell anyone until after September 2nd. I asked why.

She told me that right now, she's in her seventh week, and that September 2nd will be her twelfth week, and the chances of anything going wrong with the pregnancy after that are much slimmer. She has been on the internet in different pregnancy chat rooms with other mothers and that seems to be the general consensus. Not that she's superstitious, but I guess she's not taking any chances.

Ok, I can understand that. I don't necessarily agree with the logic, but then again, you have hormones raging throughout your body, and I've been on the receiving end of that twice before, so I'll just nod my head and smile.

She said that she hasn't really gotten any morning sickness yet, but she does feel queasy sometimes, and that she can't stand the smell of some foods. Elizabeth told me that she and Jim went to dinner at a well-known hamburger restaurant, and as soon as they walked in the door, the smell of grilled meat hit her square in the face and sent her stomach reeling. She opted for a veggie burger...at home.

We're all getting ready the next day to make the trip into the city to shop and have lunch with our son. He is one of the chosen few that will be told the secret.

Upstairs in our room, as we're getting ready, I asked my wife if Elizabeth had discussed anything else with her beyond what we talked about last night.

Without batting an eye, she replied, "Boob stuff."

"Boob stuff?", I repeat.

"Yes, boob stuff, do you want to hear about it?"

Thoughtful moment.

I replied, "Ah no, that's probably more of a mother-daughter topic, right?"

"Good call" she said.

It was a beautiful summer day. There wasn't a cloud in the sky, and a nice breeze was blowing through the trees. We all piled into the car and headed to the city.

It was a long ride. The normal forty-five minute ride ended up taking an hour and forty-five minutes. We waited in traffic for over an hour due to a detour and construction. My pregnant daughter did pretty well. She complained just once that she had to pee.

We picked up our son from his apartment and headed for a Chinese restaurant. We were all seated in a huge, horseshoe shaped booth, and made small talk while we waited for our food.

I watched my daughter for any body language that she was about to tell her brother about the impending event. Without any warning, my daughter turned to her brother and said, "Well, you're going to be an uncle."

His face froze. He slowly turned his head and grinned.

"You?"

She nodded.

*   *   *

We're now into week eleven, and the in-laws know about the impending blessed event. It was Jim's mother's birthday and everyone had gathered at their house for a cookout, and cake and ice cream. Jim's mother had called my wife and told her congratulations at the announcement. Later, Elizabeth called and went into much great detail of what happened.

Due to Elizabeth's new sickness of her stomach rolling from the smell of meat, Jim had the dubious honor of calling his mother and telling her a small white lie to bypass the hot dogs on the grill and keep Elizabeth from retching in front of the whole family. They showed up at his parents' house well after the cooking was completed and in time for the desserts. Jim, Elizabeth, Jim's parents, his grandmother, and several friends were all sitting at the table eating and his mother was opening the cards one by one.

"Dad, I was almost busting waiting for her to get to our card," said Elizabeth when I spoke with her later. "I just wanted to scream 'open our card next!'"

His mother finally got to their card.

"Gee, there's no name on this one. Did you guys pick it up at the little convenience store on the way here?" she asked.

"No Mom, I didn't. Just open the card," replied Jim.

She tore open the envelope, opened the card, and then stopped for moment. She had a somewhat puzzled look on her face as she pulled out what looked like an x-ray, but then it broke into a wide smile.

"You're going to have a baby!" she announced to the group.

Everyone gathered around with hugs and congratulations for the young couple, and looked at the ultrasound picture.

"His grandmother just sat there, her eyes were as big as saucers," said Elizabeth.

"She just kept looking back and forth at Jim and I with this big smile."

This will be Jim's parents fourth grandchild. Jim has two older brothers who both have children.

* * *

Elizabeth had her Doppler test this week, week thirteen, and called to tell us that everything was fine. Evidently the baby has my wife's temperament because the technician couldn't get the baby to cooperate. She had problems getting the baby positioned correctly to do all the necessary measurements.

Elizabeth started, "The baby is already showing that it's stubborn. The technician kept trying to maneuver it so she could measure the head, but it kept turning around."

"Sounds just like you and your father," said my wife who was listening on the other phone.

"I don't think so," Elizabeth and I both said in unison.

"Anyway," Elizabeth continued, "the technician said that the baby is about seventy-five percent head and twenty-five percent body, but around weeks twenty to twenty-two, the head stops growing and the body catches up, so when it's born, the head is twenty-five percent and the body is seventy-five percent."

"Geez, it looks like it has a watermelon head," I muttered as a peered at the shadows of my grandchild in the Doppler picture on the computer.

"That's your grandchild, so stop being mean," scolded my wife.

Elizabeth laughed. "That's ok, Jim and I were laughing because we thought it looked like an alien, but the technician said that all babies look like that at this point. We went from a plum to a peach now. She said the baby weighs three grams."

"How much is that in pounds?" I asked.

"Don't know, and I didn't ask."

Elizabeth went on.

"She was able to show us the hand, and the heart and stomach before she had to call the doctor in. The technician said they usually give it twenty minutes, and if the baby won't cooperate, then it's time to call in the doctor. The doctor shows up and, two seconds later, the baby is doing exactly what it's supposed to."

"I'm just amazed at the technology they use nowadays," said my wife. "We didn't have nearly the use of pictures like this when I was pregnant with you."

"I know, that's what everyone older has been saying," said Elizabeth. "Well, at least those who haven't been pregnant in a while."

"So, now can we tell people that we have a baby on the way?" I inquired.

"Yes Dad, you can tell people," was the reply on the other end of the phone.

The first person I had to call was my mother. My father had passed away nine years ago, and she had been living alone in the family house since, so I was hoping that the news of the next generation would be received with great joy.

I wasn't disappointed.

I was on a business trip and decided to call my mother and let her know of the great news.

"Hi Mom," I started. "I wanted to call and see how you're doing, and to share some news with you."

Right away, the Mother antennas went up.

"What kind of news?" was her first response.

"Very good news, but how are you?"

"I'm fine. What's the news?"

"Elizabeth is going to have a baby."

Silence.

"Hello?" I asked.

I then heard a loud shriek.

"This is wonderful!" my mother exclaimed. "We haven't had a baby since your brother's twins were born. I am so happy for everyone."

"Yeah, I'm going to be a grandfather. Can you believe it?" I replied.

"Well, you know, I was a grandmother at age forty-four thanks to Elizabeth. At least you're over fifty," she countered.

"I'm really happy. I knew this would be coming one day, and now, its here."

"Grandkids are great," said my mother. "You can play with them, watch them grow up, and the best part is you can send them home if they're bad. Have you told anyone else?"

"No, you're the first one. I figured I better tell you first or I'd never hear the end of it," I replied.

"You are getting smarter in your old age," my mother said and laughed.

Little did she know.

"Your brother is here. Do you want to tell him?" she asked.

"Sure, put him on," I answered.

A booming "hello" came over the receiver.

There are three brothers and one sister in my family. I am the oldest, and I was talking with my brother, Bob, who is next to me in age, and works as a diesel mechanic. Of the three brothers, he is by far the biggest. He stands at 6'3" and weighs in around 280 pounds.

"Hey Bob," I returned. "I have some news for you. Elizabeth is going to have a baby. (For some reason, I still can't bring myself to say that she's pregnant.) She's due in March."

"Oh yeah? You're going to be a grandfather."

"Yeah, I know. It hit me the first night after I was told. But you know what? You're going to be a *great* uncle. How does that sound?"

"Somehow that sounds worse. Why is that?"

"I don't know, but we're all getting old."

"You can say that again."

I finally got in touch with my youngest brother the next evening to tell him about Elizabeth. He and his wife are the parents of fraternal twin girls, Madison and Morgan, who are five. Mike is a professor at a large university in the History department.

"Hey, I've got some news for you. Elizabeth is going to have a baby. (See, I still can't say the word pregnant.) She's due in March."

A silence on the other end.

"Kim, girls, come out here. I have something to tell you," I heard him call to his family.

"Guess what?" he starts. "Your cousin Elizabeth is going to have a baby. What do you think of that?"

I could hear Kim, "Oh wow, that's great!"

The twins seemed to take the cue from their mother and started to squeal and dance around.

"Elizabeth is going to have a baby," I heard them say, almost singing it.

"So how's it feel gramps?" my brother asked. He emphasized the word *gramps*.

"Yeah, yeah, I've already dealt with that. I've got something for you. You're going to be a great uncle. Now that sounds old," I counter.

A pause.

"You're right. Man, I didn't think of that. The girls will be six when the baby is born."

"Won't be too much of an age difference between them," I said.

"You know, I'll be fifty-eight when the girls graduate high school. I'm sure people will be asking if I'm their grandfather."

"Naa, look at Linda's uncle. He was sixty when his son Tim graduated high school. Who cares?"

"Yeah, you're right. We're just all getting old."

That's the second time I've heard that phrase in the last few days.

Chapter 2

Way Too Much Information

Elizabeth is a very smart woman, sometimes too smart though. She had been doing way too much reading about pregnancy on the Internet, and as usual, much of the information dealt with the bad things that can happen during the nine months. So now, every little ache or pain that she thought was not right sent her into a tizzy that something was wrong.

Also at this point, which was week nine, she thought her mother-in-law knew about the baby. They weren't going to tell his parents until his mother's birthday in the first week of September. When Elizabeth and Jim had visited us a couple of weekends ago, Jim had mentioned to his father earlier in the week that the driver door on his car had been sticking. Well, over the weekend, his parents came to the house to look at the car. His mother went into the house and waited while his father worked on the car in the garage.

Elizabeth thought that her mother-in-law may have seen the bottle of prenatal vitamins that were sitting on the counter in the kitchen. Elizabeth said she even asked Jim if she should put the vitamins in the cupboard before they left, but both agreed that it wasn't a big deal. Well now Elizabeth thought she knows because "she's looking at me funny now." My wife did her best to calm down our daughter.

I heard my wife say several times while on the phone, "Elizabeth, I thought you weren't going to get on the computer so much to read all those articles, and talk with those other women."

One of the great things that I passed onto my daughter was the thirst for knowledge and learning. We both love to read and learn about most anything. Sometimes though, at this point, my daughter seems to have gone a little overboard. She researched everything about her pregnancy. I mean everything, which also included the bad stuff that can happen.

When she came across a symptom to be aware of, all of a

sudden Elizabeth had that ache, or pain, or rash, which then produced a call to my wife, or the doctor.

"Elizabeth, you have to calm down," my wife said.

"I know." Elizabeth said. "My logical side says that everything is fine, but my spaz side says yaaaah! I've got all these problems. You know Mom, the doctor called me back after the ultrasound. I asked him to call. I wanted to hear from him that everything was fine."

My wife responded, "Well that's good."

"I told him that my back ached, and you know what he said? Get used to it."

My wife chuckled as she hung up the phone.

"You know, you're daughter is exactly like you," she said in my general direction.

"You mean good looking, highly intelligent, and an all around great human being?" I asked.

"Well, yeah, maybe. But what I'm talking about is the need to know everything about a subject, and then having all the symptoms of every little affliction known to man."

Ouch.

"Yeah, but what about the good looking and all around great human being part?"

She looked at me and rolled her eyes.

You don't know how many times my wife has said those few words to me over the course of the last twenty-eight years. And much to her chagrin, the vast majority of people have agreed with her. My daughter and I are exactly alike.

When our daughter was born, she was the spitting image of me as a baby. As she grew into a toddler, it became more and more apparent that she looked exactly like me.

There was a time that my wife and daughter came to visit me at my office when I was in the service stationed in Virginia. I was a newly appointed Captain, and worked for the Commanding General of the base as part of the operations and protocol office just down the hall from his office. The portion of the huge hallway in the main building where the general's office was located was furnished with carpeting, dark wood, and pictures of all the previous base commanders. For some reason, Elizabeth just loved to run around on that carpet when she visited.

It was near the end of the workday, and my wife and

daughter stopped by for a quick visit on their way home from an outing. As usual, Elizabeth jumped down from my wife's arms, and began running around the carpeted hallway, her squeals and laughter echoing down the uncarpeted portion of the shiny, tiled hallway.

The general was a tall, slender, black man, very laid back, and personable. I guess when you have three stars on your collar, you can be that way. Unfortunately, in the outer office was the Chief of Staff, the guard dog who most people thought was the devil reincarnate. He had a face that looked mean without trying, was completely bald before it was fashionable, and walked with a limp, the result of an accident during his last mission as a pilot. He was now forced to sit behind a desk and deal with all the problems, both big and small, that come with running a base of twelve thousand servicemen and women.

I was chasing Elizabeth to try and scoop her up so she wouldn't make so much noise, but now it was a game to her. Being a young father, and not knowing any better, the more I chased her, the more she ran and squealed. She made a quick turn to go back up the hallway and ran right into a long pair of legs dressed in olive drab gabardine trousers. She fell back onto her behind and stared up at the tall man.

I stopped and held my breath.

By this time, several of the women who worked as administrative clerks were standing in the doorways of various offices, smiling and watching the ruckus.

The tall man leaned over and picked up Elizabeth. You could see her blue eyes get as big as saucers. My wife had just poked her head out the office door.

The tall man looked at her for moment, and turned to me, "Captain, is this your daughter?"

"Yes sir, she is."

"My God, she is your exact clone."

Clone. The name stuck.

From then on, whenever Elizabeth came to the office, she was known as *The Clone.* People would ask me how the clone was doing, or where my clone was. The name did nothing to help my wife's self-esteem either. She kept referring to herself, not as Elizabeth's mother, but simply as the *clone carrier.*

It was a good thing that our son had been born by then because he looked a little like my wife. Ok, well, he at least had darker hair like my wife.

My wife breaks my train of thought.

"Do you know what else your daughter did?"

"My daughter?"

"Yes, your daughter. She made Jim do all the vacuuming and house cleaning today because the doctor told her to take it easy for the next few days. She was actually laughing when she told me."

"Well, she gets that deviousness from you. Actually, you all learn it in wives school. I'm sure of it."

*   *   *

My daughter is a social creature. From the time she could walk, there were gaggles of girls at the house. We were the house where everyone came to play. As the years went by, and we moved to the Harrisburg, PA area, nothing changed. Ours was the house that the girls came to get dressed for the homecoming dance and prom. We were the meeting place for my daughter's annual birthday party cookout with a huge bonfire. Our driveway and yard were completely filled with cars of all years in various stages of dents and rust.

This socialization has followed my daughter into her married life. Many of her high school and college friends attended the wedding and reception following. There is a small group of them that formed a supper club that met once a month at each other's house on a rotating basis. The house that hosted the dinner is responsible for the entrée, and the visitors bring along appetizers and dessert.

On the one occasion early in her pregnancy, it was my daughter's turn to host the monthly meal. She spoke to my wife several times that week with all kinds of questions of what to prepare and how to serve it. All went well until dessert.

None of my daughter's friends were aware that she was pregnant. Remember, no one was allowed to know until after the twelfth week.

Dan and Andrea, also known as Dandrea, like the movie stars who co-join their first names, brought a decadent looking dessert. As the dessert was brought to the table, my daughter asked if there were any raw eggs used in it. No one is supposed to eat raw eggs, but I guess it's even more important for pregnant women not to eat them. The female half of Dandrea answered that no raw eggs were used.

Dessert was served and everyone dug into it. After a few bites, my daughter noticed a flavor that she had tasted before, and immediately connected it with an alcoholic beverage she consumed in her college days. She asked Andrea if there was any alcohol in the making of the dessert.

"Yeah, but just a little bit."

Elizabeth stopped chewing her last forkful and froze. She gently put down her fork, excused herself from the table, and headed upstairs.

A few minutes she came back down and retook her place at the table, chewing gum. No one said anything about her disappearance.

The rest of the meal went with no more incidents and the couples left later that evening.

While they were cleaning up, Jim asked Elizabeth why she left the table.

"I went to the upstairs bathroom and made myself throw up."

"You what?!"

"I made myself throw up."

"Why?"

"There was alcohol in the dessert. Do you want your kid coming out all stupid looking because of fetal alcohol syndrome?"

"Honey, the alcohol burns off when you cook it, and besides, it's not like you were drinking a bottle of whiskey."

"I don't care, I'm not taking any chances."

And with that, she marched upstairs and went to bed.

* * *

The phone rang and it was Elizabeth.

"Hi Dad. Did you tell grandma about the baby yet?"

"Yeah, I told her last week when I was traveling."

"Oh you did, huh?"

"Well you seemed a little reluctant to call her, so I figured I would do it. You have enough stuff to worry about."

"Oh no, it's not that. Actually I need her phone number. I'm going to call and talk with her."

My daughter holds the dubious distinction of being born on the same day as my mother, May 14th. No forgetting that birthday.

I was a green Second Lieutenant in the Marine Corps, and was scheduled to be in the field with my unit on a training exercise. Since my wife was already past her due date, she could go into labor at any time. Another lieutenant, who I had served with in the unit, and who had two children of his own, was not going out for the exercise. He agreed that he would be the relay point if my wife went into labor during the time I was in the field by sending a radio message to my unit.

We had just made an early morning move and were finishing setting up the position in the morning twilight when one of the enlisted radio operators came running towards me.

"Sir! Sir!. I just got a message from Lieutenant Wheeler. You're wife has gone into labor!"

A cheer went through the men as I grabbed my gear and jumped into the nearest jeep. The driver took me back to the command post where Lieutenant Wheeler stood ready with his car to take me to the hospital, making it in record time. I believe we broke every speed limit we came across.

I burst into the front door of the hospital and almost ran over my mother-in-law. She had arrived a few days earlier to stay with my wife while I was in the field, and to help out after the birth.

"Where's Linda?" I asked breathlessly as sweat poured off of me. I had to run a long ways from the parking lot to the hospital in the hot Carolina sun and sweltering humidity.

"Oh, they just took her back to prep her," she said.

"Prep her? I thought she was in labor," I said wiping the sweat from my forehead with my sleeve.

"Well, technically, yes she is."

My mother-in-law was a nurse in the operating room at the hospital back home, so she knew about these things.

"She's dilated about five centimeters, so the doctor asked if she wanted to have the baby today, and she said yes. So just sit down and cool off. It will be a few minutes."

I sat down in the one of the blue plastic chairs set up in the delivery waiting room. I had just noticed how nice and cool it felt in the air conditioned room after being out in the hot, humid North

21

Carolina air for several days.

A few minutes actually turned into almost an hour. A nurse came out and led me to my wife's room. Even though she had cables and several machines around her bed, she looked simply beautiful lying there. I remember thinking to myself that she looked like an angel. I sat down on the chair next to the bed and we talked quietly.

That vision was brought to a screeching halt just a few minutes later.

She had an IV hooked into her arm with a medicine to induce delivery. I was trying to keep her mind occupied and off the contraction pains by making conversation about the soap opera she was watching on the small color television mounted on the far wall.

Midway in my next sentence, I was interrupted.

"Just shut up, will you?"

I snapped my head around from the television screen and focused on my wife. The angel that had been there just a few minutes ago had been quickly replaced with a scowling, snarling creature.

"Look, I know what you're trying to do, but just shut up."

"It's the pain talking, so –." Never got to finish my sentence.

"Look, I'm warning you, just shut up," she said again.

Ok, you don't have tell me twice. I sat there quietly on my hardback chair and silently stared at the television.

It was at that time that my thoughts drifted back to the time early in my wife's pregnancy when I first found out how odd life can be with a pregnant woman. I was sitting at the small kitchen table eating breakfast at 5:30 am one morning before I headed into work. At the time, we were living in a small, rented house in the town just outside of the base. You have to understand that the bedroom was at the far end of the hallway, the door was closed, and I was sitting at the kitchen table facing away from the hallway taking a quick look at the morning paper while I ate a bowl of cereal.

I heard our bedroom door open, and out of it came, "You're crunching your cereal way too loud" and the door slammed shut.

I turned in the direction that the voice had come from and peered into the semi-darkness down the hallway. I thought for a second. Morning sickness, yep, that must be it.

At the time Elizabeth was born, it was becoming popular for fathers to be in the delivery room to be part of the whole experience. I was scheduled to do that, and had to take some sort of classes at the hospital so I could be in the delivery room, but with my work schedule of being in and out all the time, I didn't get them done, so I figured I would just chance it when the big day arrived. I didn't think the nurse at the delivery room door would be holding a clipboard with the list of fathers who had completed the pre-birth classes.

It just so happened that I was talking with another lieutenant in the unit about me being in the delivery room just few days before Linda went into the hospital. He leaned back in his chair and gave me some sage advice.

"Oh man, you don't want to be down at the business end when the baby comes," he said in a southern drawl.

"Why?" I inquired.

"Wow, it's bloody, and messy, and really gross. I made the mistake of being down there when my son was born, and almost threw up. Man, it was bad."

"Really?"

"Yeah, stay up by your wife's head. That's my advice."

"Ok, thanks."

Hmmm, something to remember.

The nurse came into the room and broke the thoughts of my memory, fiddled with some dials and wrote something on a chart, and then called for the doctor.

A few minutes later, a middle-aged, bald, pudgy man with a wide smile walked into the room. He looked at the same dials, and peered into some scope looking thing. He then put on a white rubber glove and slathered on some clear looking goop from what looked like a tube of toothpaste.

"Ok Linda, we'll check to see how much you're dilated once more, and then I think it's time to have this baby."

He bent down between my wife's spread legs, which unnerved me a little at the time, did his check and announced, "Let's head for the delivery room." He helped the nurse get the tubes and equipment unhooked, and another nurse came in to help maneuver the bed out of the room and into the hallway.

As we walked into the hall, a third nurse pulled me aside.

"Here, put these on," she said as she draped a yellow-colored paper gown over my head. She tossed me a similar yellow-colored cap to put on my head, and yellow booties for my combat boots, and I headed for the large wooden double doors marked "Delivery Room". My wife had already been escorted by several nurses through the door.

I passed through the double doors and into what seemed like another reality. You could tell right off it was a very sterile environment. My wife and her bed were placed in the middle of the tiled room with a large light above her which lit the room brilliantly. There were several nurses scurrying around working with tubes and machines. I stood off to one side trying not to get in the way.

I could hear my wife trying to do her breathing exercises, so I walked over to the bed, somewhat hesitant. I wasn't exactly sure what to do, or more importantly, what to expect. She looked at me and whispered, "Hold my hand."

I grabbed her hand and bent down close to her face.

"It's time for us to have our baby. I'll be here with you the whole time. Now just breathe."

She smiled up at me, and closed her eyes, and pushed.

The doctor walked in a few minutes later and I was little shocked at how he looked. He had on a green gown that was spattered with blood, and sneakers that looked like he had walked through a slaughter house recently.

He sat down on a stool between my wife's now propped up legs, smiling.

"Ok Linda, you're doing a good job. I can see the baby's head already. Just keep doing what you're doing."

My wife took in a deep breath.

I could hear some wet sounds coming from the area where the doctor was sitting and suddenly the previous conversation tickled my brain.

"Stay up at your wife's head."

I held Linda's hand tighter and bent closer, and coached her to breathe.

"Stay up at your wife's head."

Finally, a big wet sound, and a few seconds later, I heard a baby crying.

We made it.

After Elizabeth was born, I called my mother from the old style phone booth in the hospital to tell her that she now had a new granddaughter born on her birthday. I had rushed in from the field exercise and went right into the hospital that I forgot to call anyone and let them know. All my family knew that the first grandchild was due, but didn't know we were in the hospital.

"Hey Mom," I said into the receiver. "You have a new granddaughter. She was born just twenty minutes ago."

"Oh my God," she replied excitedly. "And on my birthday. I can't believe it!"

"Yeah, she's got ten fingers and ten toes, and she looks beautiful. Linda is doing fine as well. Everything went along like it was supposed to go."

"So her name is Elizabeth Marie?"

"Yep, Elizabeth Marie. She weighed five pounds, twelve ounces, and was nineteen inches long."

"Oh my God, I can't believe this. Our first grandchild. A beautiful, baby girl! I can't wait to see her."

A short silence.

"I've got to make a bunch of calls. Make sure you call me later."

And so the story began of Elizabeth.

It has been a stormy relationship throughout the years between my mother and my daughter since their temperaments are so much alike, but as both have aged, the relationship has been reduced to a simmer.

Back to the conversation.

"Well good, I'm sure she'll be glad to hear from you. Call me when you're done talking and let me know how it went."

I was figuring five, maybe ten minutes at the most for the whole conversation, and I'd hear back from Elizabeth. Twenty minutes went by, then thirty, and then forty-five, and yet no call back. I dialed Elizabeth's number and the phone rang and rang, and then switched over to the answering machine. I hung up without leaving a message.

Maybe she forgot to call, and is upstairs getting ready for bed.

Another twenty minutes goes by and the phone rang.

"Wow, I thought you had forgotten to call," I said.

"No, I just got off the phone with Grandma. Boy did I learn lot," Elizabeth replied.

"Oh yeah? Like what?"

"You were a big baby, over eight pounds according to Grandma. Now I'm getting a little scared."

"Scared of what?"

"I don't want to have an eight pound baby, Dad."

"I'm sure I don't have much to do with it. You and Jim are the deciding factors."

"Yeah, you're right. The doctor said that nature fits the baby to the mother. There's still a chance I could have a bigger baby, but standing at four feet, ten inches, and one hundred ten pounds, I'm thinking probably not."

"I agree. What else did you guys talk about?" I asked as I searched for any hint of turbulence.

"Did you know that Grandma had spotting during her pregnancies too?"

"No, I don't think I knew that," as I tried to keep any mental pictures out of my head.

"I didn't know this, but Grandma had a miscarriage before Uncle Mike was born."

"I knew that. Some years ago, when I was still in college, we ended up talking about it. Actually I think it was Grandpa and I."

We talked about the baby's room, and Jim's parents, and baby names."

"Names? Like what?"

"Well, I said that I didn't like the more popular names now like Bryce, or Dylan, and for girls, Amanda or Emily."

"You have some time to think about names. So it was a good conversation?"

"Oh yeah, I enjoyed it. I told her I'd call again sometime soon."

"Good," I said. "I'm sure she enjoyed the conversation as well. You should talk with her every so often. She'd like to hear from you."

"I will Dad. Honest."

"Good, now go get some sleep. Pregnant women need all the sleep they can get, ya know?"

*   *   *

It was early on a Saturday morning in the fall. I was up

26

getting my uniform and other items ready for a high school football game I had later that afternoon. I had been an official for high school football for the last twelve years. The phone rang, and the name came up on the caller id as 'PA Cell Phone' and I almost didn't answer it, but it kept ringing, and finally I grabbed it so it didn't disturb Linda.

I said hello and waited for some faceless person on the other end to start reciting a memorized sales pitch.

"Hey Dad," said Elizabeth. "What's up?"

"Well, what are you doing up so early on a Saturday?" I inquired.

"Oh I woke up at 7:00 am this morning and couldn't go back to sleep, so I just got up."

"What's Jim doing?"

"He's upstairs in the shower."

"So what can I do for you"? I asked, knowing that there had to be another reason for Elizabeth to call so early on a Saturday.

"I wanted to talk over something with you. Jim and I went out to eat last night at our favorite Friday night restaurant. We met Bruce and Jill there, and ended up having wings. There are so good. I had the honey barbecue wings, and then we had some crème brulee. Crème brulee has eggs in it, and I kept asking Jill if there were any raw eggs in it."

"Well that sounds good, always pays to be cautious," I replied waiting for her to circle around to the point.

"Well, the thing is…I had diarrhea a couple times last night, and again this morning. Do you think its food poisoning?"

I rolled my eyes.

"No Elizabeth, it's not food poisoning. I've seen people with food poisoning, and if you had it, you would be doubled over in pain. Doesn't sound like you are."

"No, I didn't think so either. I looked it up online this morning, and I don't have all the symptoms. I think it was the food from last night."

Way too much information at her fingertips.

"I would agree with you. Think about it. You've hardly eaten anything at all over the past month because you get nauseous, and then all of a sudden, you have wings and crème brulee. That would upset a goat's digestive system."

Elizabeth laughed. "I know, I thought the same thing, but I

guess I wanted to hear from you or Mom. Did she tell you what we bought?"

"You mean the car seat and carrier?"

"Yeah, it's really nice. It's a charcoal, ivory, and chrome color scheme."

Oh boy.

"Jim and I took it out of the box last night. We just both looked at each other not knowing the first thing about it."

Car seats. That brings back a memory.

We had been in the unit for just about a year when Elizabeth was born. My wife had made some close friends with other wives in that time and they all looked after each other. Everyone was in the same situation with husbands coming and going, so you learned to rely on one another for support. That's one of the really great things about the military. There's a closeness that you can't explain to someone who has not experienced it.

When Linda and Elizabeth were ready for discharge from the hospital the next day, I brought the car around with my mother-in-law in the back seat, and opened the door. My wife was seated comfortably in a wheel chair at the curb holding our new daughter.

The burly nurse, and I say that with all sincerity, stood with her hands on her hips behind the wheelchair.

"Where's the car seat?" she demanded in a deep voice.

"Oh,...well...I haven't put it in yet," I replied.

"This baby and new mother are not putting one foot in that vehicle until the car seat is hooked up," she announced.

I ran around to the trunk of the car and opened the lid. We had bought a stand-by car seat because the other had not arrived yet. I pulled out the box, tore it open, and wrestled the car seat from the box. I stared at the contraption. It may as well have been a rocket engine because I had about the same level of knowledge of either at that point.

"Well, do you know how to install it?" the nurse asked, her meaty arms now folded across her ample bosom.

"Um" was all I could come up with.

She moved quickly for a woman of her bulk, and came around the wheelchair and snatched the seat from my hands. In thirty seconds, she had it hooked, tethered, strapped, tied and bolted to the car.

"Now, did you see how I did that?"

My first thought was how could I when you're large enough to block out the sun, but I managed to reply with a feeble "yes."

My wife tenderly put Elizabeth into the car seat and strapped her in. We paused to take in the sight. Elizabeth was just a tad under six pounds, so she actually looked like a child's doll sitting in the car seat.

I shook my head and the memory disappeared.

"Been there myself," I replied. "You guys got anything planned for the weekend?"

"We're actually getting ready to go to Washington D.C for an Oktoberfest with Dan and Andrea. Dan and Jim bought these tickets to taste beer from all around the world."

"Didn't Andrea get a ticket?" I ask.

"No, they're trying to get pregnant, so she's not drinking at all."

Whoa, I probably didn't need to know that part.

"At least you'll have another non-drinker with you to keep you company."

Just then, I heard Linda come down the stairs.

"Hey, your mother just came downstairs. Want to talk with her?"

"Sure," came her reply.

"Be careful on your trip, and let us know how it went. Love you"

"We will, and love you too."

I called to my wife who is in the kitchen preparing her morning tea, "You're favorite daughter would like to talk with you."

A response from the phone, "I'm your only daughter, Dad."

I handed over the phone to my wife. For the next several minutes, I listened to my wife ask the same basic questions I did.

She hung up the phone and came into the living room and sat down with her cup of tea.

"Did she tell you she thought she may have food poisoning?" she asked, shaking her head.

"Yes she did," I replied. "But I talked her off the ledge and now everything is fine."

"What does she think would happen with eating wings and crème brulee after a month of cereal and bread?"

"I don't know. She's your daughter."

* * *

One of the major sticking points with Elizabeth since she found out she was pregnant has been a car. I can't say as I blame her. Her car was a 1998 Honda with over 120,000 miles on it. She bought the car during her junior year in high school and worked odd jobs to pay for it and her insurance. I co-signed the car for her, but was little hesitant at the time because she had never taken on such a big task before. I was pleasantly surprised in that she never missed payment or asked for help from her mother or I.

Ok, there was a three month time period when she got a little emotional and quit her job with nothing as a back-up, but we'll put that under the category of a life experience.

Some would say that there are a lot of miles left on the car, and that a Honda is well-known for being reliable well over 200,000 miles. I would agree with you on those points, but it's a two door stick shift. Not the perfect car to be hauling around a baby in a car seat.

It must be the genetics again. Several months before Linda and I got married, I had just gotten my first brand new car, a 1980 Pontiac Grand Prix. It was metallic maroon, had a white landau roof, and was just beautiful. In fact, the retired woman who lived across the street from my in-laws was so enamored with the car when she saw it on the weekends when I visited, she went out and bought one exactly like it.

When Elizabeth came along, my wife felt that the Pontiac became somewhat impractical. It was a great car, but it also was a two-door, and back then, the doors were big and heavy. They were a pretty tough task for my one hundred pound wife to get open and closed.

So bye, bye sleek, powerful man-mobile; hello four-door family car. And the rest, as they say, is history.

So here is Elizabeth, five months pregnant, with a ten year old car. Jim's car was not any better. He inherited his car from his grandmother a few years ago. It was a 1993 sedan that had certainly seen better days. It was reliable transportation, if you didn't mind the purple hue, but the basics like door locks didn't necessarily work all the time.

I offered a solution that they just switch cars. Jim's was a four-door sedan, so that should have worked. I found out that there was a big issue. Jim couldn't drive a stick. I guess he had tried to learn, but to no avail. On to the more expensive solution.

Elizabeth had set her sights on a mini-van, but Jim was dead set against it. Evidently they made a compromise, as all good couples do, and were now focused on an SUV.

Elizabeth called on Saturday to tell us about her car shopping trip with Jim in the search for the perfect SUV.

"Dad, it was so scary. I was driving a brand new car worth $25,000. I've never done that before. And to make matters worse, I had to keep reminding myself that it was an automatic. A couple of times I tried to push in the clutch only to remember there wasn't one."

I chuckled.

"I've done that myself. I remember when I got my first new car. I was so used to pushing in the clutch that the car sales guy riding with me laughed as I searched for the pedal."

"I know. This guy didn't say anything, but I'm sure he saw me searching for the clutch."

"That's ok. What did you think of it?" I inquired.

"Oh, it was so nice. It was really quiet compared to my car, and it had all these really neat gadgets on it."

I could hear the excitement in her voice.

"So, did you buy it?"

"No, we just went looking. It was so hard not to buy it. Did you know that you're really not supposed to say anything about a trade-in until you make the deal?"

"Yeah, I think somewhere I heard that."

"We talked with Jim's dad before we went, and he told us all these things to do and not do. He knows all about it since he works with various car dealers."

"Can he get me a brand new BMW with no payments?"

"No Dad, he's not that kind of car guy. You know that."

"So, what's the next step?"

"Well, there are two more dealerships Jim wants to go to, and then he'll sit down and crunch the numbers as he says. After that, it's the one with the best deal for the best car. Cool, huh?"

"Yep, cool."

Elizabeth called last night to give us the latest update on their car search. The calls always seemed to come around bedtime, the part of the day when you want to take a nice, hot shower and relax in bed maybe watch some tv program, or read a good book. But since we don't get to see them very often, a call at any time of the day or night from Elizabeth was ok.

I was laying sideways on the bed watching a football (on mute) while Linda gabbed on and on with Elizabeth on her cell phone. I heard that they had gone to several other dealers to get more information on vehicles, and Jim was now looking at all the information to find the best deal.

"Did you know that you now haggle over car prices online?" I heard Elizabeth say.

"What do you mean haggle online?" asked Linda.

"Now, each car dealership has a person that works online and does all the negotiating with you. We have now moved into the haggling portion of the deal."

"Did you find the car you wanted?"

"No," came Elizabeth's reply. "No one has the vehicle we wanted. That also works in our favor though. We wanted a two-wheeled drive SUV, but all they have are four-wheeled drive. Maybe we can get them down on a price for a four-wheeled drive car at a two-wheeled drive price."

"You know," started her mother, "you really won't use the four-wheeled drive all that often. We've had our SUV for six years and I've used the four-wheeled drive maybe a handful of times. I remember I had to call your father on how to put it in four-wheeled drive the first time I used it."

It was one of those weeks when Linda and I were traveling in opposite directions. I had to go on a business trip from Harrisburg to Pittsburgh, and she was traveling to see her Dad in north central PA. Even though she was traveling north and I was traveling west, we both ran into a snow storm at about the same time.

I was traveling in a company car on the Pennsylvania Turnpike in the mountains when the snowstorm struck. It was night and visibility was very bad. I was trying to negotiate the curves and hills while staying on the road when my cell phone rang. Probably the smartest thing to do was to pull over and take the call, but the snow was falling so thick that I was concerned about getting stuck. And I've been accused of many things, but being the smartest was never one of them.

I recognized the number as Linda's and flipped open the phone.

"Hey, what's going on?" I said into the phone.

"I need your help," came my wife's voice from the other end. "I'm on a small stretch of Interstate 80, it's icy, and I'm having trouble getting up the hills. How do you put this thing in four-wheeled drive?"

I thought back. I don't think I had ever actually used four-wheeled drive on Linda's car, but I had a faint memory of reading about it in the owner's manual. I tried to remember how I did it in our old SUV, and pictured the car's layout in my mind.

"Ok, do this. Put the gearshift in neutral," I said as I peered through the windshield into the thick snow lit by the headlight beams.

"Done."

"Good. Find the lever next to it and move it from two-wheel high to four-wheel low. It's a little tough, so you're going to need to push hard."

"Alright, I'm going to need both hands, so I'm going to put down the phone."

I heard unrecognizable noises, a dull mechanical grinding, and then silence.

"Ok, it's in four-wheel drive."

"Good. Now with your foot still on the brake, put the gearshift into drive, and you should be good to go."

A few seconds went by.

"Woohooo!" I heard Linda shout in the phone. "This is really cool. I'm going right up the hill while everyone else is stuck. I'll call you later, bye."

And the phone went dead.

We both managed to make it to our destinations unscathed, and laugh about it now.

"So you see, I wouldn't have the four-wheeled drive make it a deal breaker Elizabeth," explained Linda.

"Oh, I know. I'll just wait to see how it all works out. Jim's concerned that if we have a big car payment, and something goes wrong with his car, we'll be a one car family."

"Elizabeth, you do what you have to do. Remember when your father first got out of the military? We were a one car family for the first couple of years after having two cars for ten years."

"Yeah, I remember getting up at 5:30 in the morning and riding in with you guys taking Dad into work. It's funny. When we asked Jim's Dad about it, he said the same thing. Do what you got to do."

"See, so don't sweat it. So how are you feeling?"

"Gosh Mom, I think I got a small taste today of what labor might be like."

Linda laughed. "What do you mean?"

"You know that ever since I've been pregnant, I've been pretty constipated. I've been drinking a glass of prune juice in the morning and that seems to help a little. Today though, it just got so bad that I had to go in and try. I'm in the bathroom on the pot and pushing as hard as I can."

Linda started to laugh hysterically.

"I'm holding on to the sides, pushing as hard as I can, and I see stars, and get light-headed. A thought raced through my mind that Jim would come home after work and find me slumped on the bathroom floor passed out with my pants down around my ankles," Elizabeth said between bouts of laughter.

Linda laughed so hard the bed shook.

"Oh gosh Elizabeth, what are we going to do with you?" replied Linda after she got her breath back.

"The best part," Elizabeth continued, "is that I did have success and stopped up the toilet. I had to get the plunger and work it free. It took me some time, but now all is good."

Another round of laughter.

"Oh, and tell Dad that the baby is the size of a small doll. It's pretty much looks like how it will be when its born, it will fill out and gain weight between now and then."

"Hey," Linda said to me as I lay on the bed. "You daughter says that the baby is now the size of a small doll."

"Great," I replied, not moving.

"Not much response from your Dad. You know it is after 10 pm. Well after his bedtime."

"Yeah, he can't hang with the girls," retorts Elizabeth.

"Whatever," I said along with a wave of my hand. "Shouldn't all pregnant women be in bed by now? Make sure my grandchild gets all the needed rest?"

"Yeah, you're probably right, but I go into work late tomorrow," explained Elizabeth. "We have a guy coming out to check the furnace."

"Wonderful. Good night Elizabeth."

"Good night Dad."

*   *   *

The house was quiet. Linda had a dinner meeting at the church with her woman's group, so I was left to fend for myself. After heating up some leftover chicken and rice, I went into the living to eat while watching some tv. Just as I was finishing my supper, Linda's cell phone rang. It was Elizabeth.

"Hey Dad, what are you doing?" she started.

"Just finishing up some leftover chicken and rice for supper," I answered.

"Sounds like us. We just finished up some leftover meatloaf. I didn't feel like cooking."

"So what can I do for my best daughter?"

"Remember, I'm your only daughter. Actually I called to complain to Mom."

"Oh yeah? Well your mother is at a church women's meeting, so you'll have to complain to me."

"That's right. She did tell me that."

"So what are you complaining about?" I inquired.

"I now officially have cankles," she announced. "You know, no ankle. It goes from calf muscle to foot."

"Well, you are gaining weight, so I'm sure it's putting more pressure on your joints now."

"No," she said, "This is not just cankles, this is gross cankles. I didn't even notice them until I put my feet up on the couch tonight. I looked down and saw how gross they were. It's too early for this."

"Well," I began. "There's not a whole lot you can do about it. Maybe you should ask the doctor the next time you're in."

"Yeah, maybe I should be using less salt. I don't know."

"Hey Elizabeth, you know what? Your mother made two apple pies today for the dinner meeting tonight, and she made a small one out of the leftover dough and apples she had. As soon as you and I hang up, I'm having a big piece of it.

"Don't say anything about sweets. I have a glucose test tomorrow and haven't been able to have any sweets today."

"What's the glucose test for?" I asked.

"It's to check for gestational diabetes. You have to drink this icky stuff and then they draw blood after one hour to see how well your body is taking care of the sugar. If I fail this one, I have to go back for a three hour test where they draw blood every hour for three hours."

"I don't think I'd like that one," I replied.

"No, I don't think I'd like that one either. You know how well I do with needles. Remember Cindy who was in my wedding? She craved orange soda pop when she was pregnant, and drank a lot of it just before her glucose test. No one said she couldn't. I guess when the results came back, she was off the chart. She had to go back and do the three hour test and passed that one."

"Wow, all these tests."

"This is my last one. After this, I just have my regular appointments. And then after Christmas, I start having them every two weeks."

"Getting closer, huh?"

"Yep. This time next year, things will be a lot different," she said laughingly.

"Elizabeth, you don't know what you don't know yet. Believe me," I said softly.

After several days of no phone calls from Elizabeth, we now had several days of calls each day. Also not unusual, she was spazing about something with each call.

It was just after I had come downstairs from work, and Linda had supper in the oven, and we were watching the news. Her cell phone rang and she picked it up to look at who was calling.

"Ah oh, it's your daughter," she said quietly.

"Is there a problem I should know about?" I inquired.

She answered the phone and spoke with Elizabeth for almost half an hour. I was pretty engrossed in listening to the news about the recent earthquake in Haiti, so I wasn't really paying much attention to her talking, but I did pick up phrases like "calm down" or "you don't need that right away."

Linda closed her phone, and put it on the end table between our chairs. She got up out of the chair and started for the kitchen.

"I don't know what we're going to do with our spaz child. I hope she makes it," she said as she shook her head.

"Why, what's going on?" I asked as I followed her into the

kitchen. I was hungry and wanted to look for something to gnaw on before dinner.

"Remember she invited Jim's parents over for dinner tonight?"

"Yeah," I said somewhat absentmindedly as I leaned into the refrigerator and moved things around.

"What are you doing?"

"I'm hungry, and I wanted something before dinner."

"Get out of there. We'll be eating in ten minutes. You can wait that long."

I closed the door to the refrigerator and leaned up against the counter. Bad boy.

"Why, what's up?" I asked.

"They had invited Jim's parents over for dinner tonight. She was making some sort of chicken dish where you make a brine solution and then marinate it for 24 hours."

"That doesn't sound too difficult," I interjected.

She held up one finger. "Wait, there's more."

So I sat down in one of the kitchen chairs and waited for the rest of the story.

"They got home late last night since they had the baby class at the hospital, and she still had to make the marinating solution. She said she thought about just doing a different recipe because it was so late, but decided to go ahead with her original idea. So she get's out her food processor and puts together all the stuff for the marinade."

"The same processor we have?" I asked.

"No, theirs is bigger, now listen. She looks at all the liquid in the processor and decides that it's too full. She takes off the lid and is going to scoop out some of it, and she accidently hits the pulse button."

"Oh God, I remember when I did that while making a protein shake."

"She said that the marinade flew everywhere...all over the counter, dripped down the cupboard doors, on the ceiling, and all over the floor. She said she just stood there and looked around, and could feel some of the sauce on her face as it slowly trickled down her chin. And she said, 'Mom, I just started to cry. I don't know why, but I started crying.'"

"Where was Jim?"

"He was upstairs taking a shower. So she cried for a bit, and then calmed down. She started to clean up the mess, and at this point is down on her hands and knees scrubbing the floor. She said the stuff was everywhere, and it was so hard to get off because the garlic and lemon juice made it like cement. She said that Jim came downstairs and saw her, and asked what she was doing. She said she started to explain, and began crying again."

"Aw, see I wish we were closer to help her with stuff like that."

"So Jim tells her to go upstairs and take a nice hot shower, and that he would finish up cleaning and making the marinade. See, what a nice guy."

"Yep, I guess you and your daughter can pick them, huh?"

A few moments of stunned silence, and then she continued.

"After dinner tonight, Jim's mother wanted to look at the list of things Elizabeth had picked on Amazon.com for her shower. Elizabeth said to go ahead and look, but she didn't want to because then she would then know what people had gotten her."

Just then, the timer on the microwave oven beeped. Linda opened the oven door, moved some of the chicken around in the pan, and closed the oven door. She put five minutes on the timer and started it. The aroma of the baking chicken smelled wonderful as it filled the kitchen. It was hard to concentrate.

"Jim's mother was looking through the list and made a comment that there were still a lot of things left on the list. Well, you know your daughter, that got her curious and she started looking through the list as well."

"Oh geez, now what?" I asked as I silently watched the timer numbers slowly descending.

"Now she's all upset that there are a bunch of things left on the list that she needs. She was saying that she needs the high chair, and she needed this and needed that. Half the stuff she was taking about she won't need until the baby gets a little older."

"It's that nesting instinct, you know."

"Oh great. Way to be Mr. Sensitivity," Linda shot back.

"What? It's a well know fact that the nesting instinct becomes stronger the closer a woman gets to the baby's time. Look at how we wrestled with the changing table just days before Elizabeth arrived."

I had come home from work one day, and as I was coming

through the garage into the kitchen, I noticed a beat-up three drawer dresser sitting off to one side. It wasn't there when I had left for work that morning.

I came into the kitchen and Linda was sitting in the easy chair with her feet up. Her due date was a month or so away.

"Hey, how are you feeling?" I asked as I kissed her on the forehead.

"Ok, I just needed to get off of my feet for a few minutes. Did you happen to notice anything in the garage?"

"If you mean that beat up dresser that is painted brown, then yes. Where did it come from?"

"I went shopping with Dee today and we stopped at an antiques place. I saw this dresser, and really liked it, and it was just fifty dollars. I thought we could redo it and make it a changing table for the baby."

Notice the word *we?*

Dee was our next door neighbor, and was married to a Lieutenant Colonel in the Marine Corps. They had adopted us after we had moved in, and had four kids who were all older. I think the youngest was a junior in high school. They really helped us get acclimated to North Carolina as a newly married couple in the Marine Corps.

"Let me take a look at it," I said as I headed back out the kitchen door to the garage.

I pulled the dresser away from the wall and walked around it. There was a large, raggedy crack between the boards on the one side; the hardware would have to be replaced; there were dents in the wood; and the painted brown color was hideous. I really didn't think there was a whole lot I could do for it. This was my first attempt at refinishing anything.

Linda was standing in the kitchen doorway watching me. "Well, what do you think?"

"I'll see what I can do, but I'm not making any promises."

For the next week, the dresser sat on a large bed sheet in our nearly empty family room. I stripped off the brown paint and took it right down to the bare wood. I was surprised to see that it was maple. I sanded out the dents in the top.

"Will it be ready before the baby comes?"

I was able to borrow a couple of wood clamps from the Colonel next door, and glued the boards together that were cracked.

"Do you think you'll have it done before the baby?"

I put a nice coat of maple stain on it followed by several coats of polyurethane. Linda bought new handles for the drawers and I installed them.

"Boy honey, this is getting close. Will it be ready?"

It was a lot of late nights, but in the end, we had a beautiful looking changing table. And it wasn't too soon.

"I think it's time to go to the hospital."

I'm not sure the final coat of polyurethane was dry when Elizabeth came into the world. A couple of years later, a repairman for the furnace saw the dresser sitting in the baby's room, and offered Linda $250 for it. Not bad for a first try.

"So I tried to calm her down," Linda said. "I'm not sure I did a very good job."

"Why? What was there to get stressed about?"

"She said that no one had picked out the high chair, or a couple of the others in the high dollar stuff. I told her that people may be looking at the stuff in the stores, or waiting until it gets a little closer to the shower and going in on them together. People still have a couple of weeks yet. She kept going on and on about how everything that's not picked yet will cost a thousand dollars, and that she needs it now."

"Wow, they don't need all new stuff. Do they?"

"No, I don't think so, but your daughter certainly does."

"I wonder where she gets that?" I asked as I stared at Linda.

"Hey, if you remember, we did a lot of our stuff with used and hand-me-downs."

"Oh, I remember that, but it was all the stuff afterwards that had to be new."

The timer beeped again. Dinner, finally.

"Elizabeth said that they were going over to Jim's parents. They had gotten the stroller and wanted to put it together."

"It's a good thing that Jim's dad is handy with that kind of thing. I was never very good at that. You need a PhD to read the directions," I replied.

"No, not a PhD, just a little mechanical aptitude," she said as she patted me on top of the head.

My turn for stunned silence.

Chapter 3

Some Bumps In The Road

As with any new addition, buildings, people, or otherwise, there are usually some bumps in the road. At the time, it seems as if it won't end, but looking back on it, it really was a short time. We went through our fair share of bumps with Elizabeth and the baby. It seemed as if every day there was something wrong, a pain here, or a spot there. I certainly don't remember all this fuss with either of my kids. My wife tells me it's because I was gone a lot during that time and she took care of it. Typical female response.

I had just gotten off the phone with my wife. Our daughter had some bleeding one morning and sounded general quarters. She called the doctor and he had her come right in. My stomach was churning and I had that bottomless pit feeling.

This is my first pregnancy as a grandfather, and I'm not sure how to react. It was only week eight.

I was getting this all information second-hand from my wife because I was in Kansas City on a business trip. My wife is tough, but I heard the sniffles on the other end. She was also dealing with the death of a close aunt that she found out about just after I landed in Kansas City. She's a lot better at handling this kind of stuff than I am. She's been my rock for over twenty-eight years. I'd be a quivering, human gelatin mold without her.

She has just spoken with our daughter who said that everything is fine.

The doctor said that four out of ten pregnancies have some sort of bleeding or spotting associated with them. He had our daughter complete an ultrasound and they took pictures of the little bean. The ultrasound technician said that they use some form of vegetable to make a comparison of how big the baby is. In this case, a pinto bean is the choice vegetable.

I breathed a sigh of relief, and my wife and I laughed about it. I told her that we are good Pennsylvania frontier stock, and that our daughter is no different. She and the baby will be fine.

My daughter and the baby crossed my mind several times during the day. Just to hear it from her, I decided to call my daughter later that night. I hesitated because I wondered if the conversation was going to upset her. I thought about it for a few minutes as I sat watching a baseball game on tv. Since I was on a business trip, I got to watch what I wanted.

I made the decision to call her. I picked up the phone and punched in the number. It rang...and rang...and rang.

Finally, after what seemed an intolerable time, she answered and I heard her cheerful voice on the other end, "Hey Dad."

We talked for several minutes, reliving the situation from the morning.

She told me that the ultrasound technician took pictures and gave them to her. She will try to scan them into the computer and send them to me. She also described to me that they were able to hear the baby's heartbeat...*ba-thoomp, ba-thoomp*...183 times a minute. The technician also told her that a heartbeat count of 120-200 are normal and that everything was working as it should.

"I cried at that point, Dad. I think it was more out of relief than anything else."

"Well, I can understand that. It would be a tough thing for anyone to go through," I said back to her.

"You know Dad; I saw some tears in Jim's eyes as well. He said that it was at that point that the baby became very real to him. He kept saying all the way home 'Look, that's our baby'."

"Well, this is a big event for the both of you. You should take a break from the gym and your work out activities, or at least reduce them," I said in my best fatherly voice.

She reassured me that she will not going to do anything for the rest of the week, and that she is going to just rest.

I agreed with her.

* * *

I spoke with my wife the next night on the phone and she described the funeral for her aunt and the happenings at the family get-together afterwards. The gathering was at my in-law's house which was recently put on the market to be sold after the death of my father-in-law. That was a difficult decision for my wife and her brother, but a story for another time.

The lone remaining brother on my wife's maternal side, Larry, from California, came with his wife to be at the funeral. Larry and his wife, Nancy, are really great people and visit a couple of times each year.

"I think Nancy is psychic," my wife said.

"Why do you say that?" I asked.

"Well, we were sitting there talking and she says something like 'it's time for Elizabeth and Jim to have a baby, right?' I almost choked on my sandwich."

"So what's the big deal? Everyone has been saying that since Elizabeth got married," I replied.

"Remember the time you and I had set up that trip to Chicago to look at houses when you were thinking about transferring there with the company?"

"Yeah and…"

"At Mom's family reunion the week before we left, she asked us when we were moving to Chicago, remember?"

"Yeah, as a matter of fact, now that you say that, I do."

Nancy is from Chicago, and it was eerie how her question came out right at that time. It was such an unexpected question that my wife and I stammered around with an answer, and we ended up spilling everything right then of our potential plans.

"When I told Elizabeth about it, she asked the same question, if Nancy was psychic."

"You know, she is part Indian, I think Cherokee, and some say they are psychic," I tease.

"Oh, very funny, Mr. Know-It-All."

Geez, how many more days before we can start talking about this?

* * *

Elizabeth called again the following week and sounded more alarmed than usual. It seems she had some more spotting, went over the top again, and called her mother and the doctor. The doctor set her up for an appointment the next day; I'm sure more to appease her than any other real reason. He reassured her on the phone that the tests and ultrasound that were done last week

43

showed everything was fine. He will do another ultrasound to check the baby's heartbeat.

He also told her that brown blood is ok, because it means its old blood and nothing to be concerned about. If it was bright red, then there may be a problem, but this is nothing out of the ordinary.

I talked to Elizabeth on the phone. I tried to reassure her that everything was going to be fine. She kept saying over and over that she was scared, and she didn't want anything to happen. I told her that nine months is a long time, and there are going to be more ups and downs, so you might as well get use to it.

Mid-conversation, my wife's cell phone went dead. A few minutes later, Elizabeth called back on the house phone and her mother answered. They talked for a few minutes, but since Elizabeth had gone back to work, they made it short.

My wife hung up the phone and let out a big sigh.

"I don't know what we're going to do," she said. "I won't be able to take this for nine months. She'll drive us all crazy."

"Did you check to see if she wants us to come out for a few days?" I asked.

"She said not to worry about it until she gets the results back from the doctor's appointment tomorrow."

We had no more calls that day, but it was a restless night. My wife was awake for a good portion of the night pacing around the house and worrying about Elizabeth. When that happens, I can't sleep because then I am concerned about my wife. Finally, around 2 am, my wife came back into bed and we were able to get some rest.

The phone rang around 10 am and it was Elizabeth. She had gone to the doctor and had the check-up. They did a procedure using a Doppler that is usually done later in the pregnancy. The doctor said that the heartbeat was strong and that everything looked very good. It's not unusual for first-time pregnancies to have spotting or a small amount of bleeding. They told Elizabeth to call only if the blood was bright red and she had cramping.

Sounded like the doctor was giving Elizabeth orders.

I could hear my wife on the phone downstairs. "See, I told you everything would be ok. Now, are you calmer? Good, don't let yourself get so upset."

Another catastrophe avoided. Until the next one.

The autumn flew by, and it was soon Thanksgiving. When I was a kid, Thanksgiving was always a special time because family would come over, we'd all eat a big meal, and then watch football. Since I've had my family, and being in the military stationed all over the country, we rarely made it back to our parents' homes for the holiday. After I got out of the service, and we lived in Harrisburg, it was a four to five hour trip to parents' houses, and Linda and I usually had to work on the Friday after Thanksgiving. Few trips were made back for that holiday. Now that my kids are grown and out of the house, I have a better understanding of how difficult it is for them to get back to our house for the holiday.

Our son will be here for the day since he lives just forty-five minutes away from us. Elizabeth, however, won't be making the trip this year. She and Jim are traveling with Jim's parents to the middle brother's house in Virginia to celebrate the holiday. Being six months pregnant and somewhat uncomfortable, I'm sure Elizabeth would rather stay at home, but she is a trooper.

Linda's cell phone rang last night, and I picked it up in the kitchen. A picture of Chloe the devil cat appeared on the small screen. It was Elizabeth calling. I flipped open the phone.

"Hey girlie, what's up?"

"Hi Dad, what are you doing?"

"Watching a football game."

"Gee, I'm not surprised," came her reply. "It's Tuesday. Who's playing tonight?"

"It's a Division Two game. Ball State and Western Michigan on ESPN2."

"Geez Dad, that's all you seem to do is watch football."

"No, no, no little girl," I started. "I worked all day so I can keep your mother in the luxury living that she's become accustomed to, went to the gym and worked out, did a few chores around the house to help your mother, and I just sat down a few minutes ago. So how's that?"

"Yeah, yeah. I've heard that before. Hey, I called to talk with Mom about the crib."

"She just went upstairs to take shower. Let me see if I can catch her before she gets in. Hey, I just thought of something. Why don't you name the baby Espn, you know, like the sports channel? I've heard that other people have done that."

45

Silence on the other end.

"Ok, I take that as a no. Boy, you have no creativity."

I lifted my tired and somewhat sore body out of the 'Dad' chair and started up the stairs.

"So," I said, "I hear you're traveling south for the holiday."

"Yeah, and you know what? We're leaving at 7:15 am. I'll have to get up at six."

"Well, that's what you have to do sometimes for family," as I tried to reason with her.

"I don't mind traveling for the holiday, but Jim just told me that we're not coming back until late Saturday."

"Ok, so you come back on Saturday night. Relax. What's the big deal?"

"What's the big deal?" she said, her voice rising.

I sensed she was getting wound up.

"I was hoping to have a day or two to relax, because you know I am six months pregnant. I have to clean the house on Sunday, and I wanted to put up the Christmas decorations too. Where am I going to find the time to do all those things?"

Ok, time to switch to Dad mode.

"Elizabeth, don't put so much pressure on yourself. So the house doesn't get cleaned on Sunday, no big deal. Do a little each night. Do the same with the decorations. Break it up into something to get done each evening after supper."

Silence on the other end.

"What does Jim have to say about all this?" I inquired.

"I'm not talking to him right now," was her short reply.

"Why?"

"He won't say anything to his parents, that's why."

Oh boy, I've been in this place before. Wife wants one thing (rock) and the parents want another thing (hard place), and I'm right between them.

"Elizabeth, it's ok. Relax, this is going to happen whether you get upset or not. Embrace it and make the most of it."

A short pause.

"You're right," she said. "I'm very tired right now. I didn't sleep very well last night and I'm letting it get to me."

"Yeah, things will look better in the morning," I reassure her.

"No they won't, but I won't be as tired," she said with a

chuckle.

Linda had been sitting on the cedar chest in our bedroom listening to our conversation.

"Ok, here's you mother. I'm sure she dying to talk with you," I said as I winked at Linda.

She mouthed 'Oh thanks.'

I handed the phone over to Linda and took a long, hot shower. It felt great after an unusually hard day.

I came out of the bathroom as Linda was hanging up with Elizabeth.

"You know," she said, "I can relate to what Elizabeth said. Whenever we traveled as a family, I tried to get us back so we could have a day or two to relax before we went back to work, or the kids went back to school. I think everyone needs time to chill out."

"Yeah, I agree. That's something they'll have to work out though."

"Oh yeah, and they will," she reasoned. "You and I did," she whispered as she reached out and gently tweeked my nose on her way to the bathroom.

"So what did Elizabeth want about the crib?" I called out to her.

Linda and I had agreed that we would get the baby's crib for Elizabeth and Jim. We had told them about it during our last visit. Ok, I told them about the crib only to find out later from Linda that I wasn't supposed to. Of course, a brand new, name brand crib now costs over $400 after you add in all the amenities.

Times certainly have changed. I don't remember it being like this when we were going to have Elizabeth. We bought a used crib from my battalion commander for $25 and both kids slept in it. No problem.

Maybe it's not the times that have changed, more like my daughter's tastes.

Linda stuck her head out of the bathroom doorway.

"She just wanted to let us know that she changed the type of crib she wanted. With all recalls happening now with cribs, she was concerned, so she went with another brand."

"And I'm guessing it's more expensive, right?"

"Only $50 more."

Yeah, only $50.

Thanksgiving came and went this past week. We had a small family gathering at the house which included my mother, my son, and my brother's family. As usual, my wife made way too much food, but we all gave a mighty effort in trying to make it disappear.

Elizabeth and Jim had gone with Jim's parents to Richmond to spend the holiday with his brother's family. We actually didn't hear from Elizabeth until Saturday. We did get a text message wishing us a happy Thanksgiving at around 9:30 on Thursday morning, and then a quick call to let us know that they made it safely.

As usual, Elizabeth called around the time when Linda was in the shower, so I ended up talking with her for a quite a while in hearing about her trip.

"The trip itself wasn't bad," she started. "I slept for part of the way which made it go much faster. The big thing is that we didn't leave until eight that morning. I got to sleep in another hour."

"Got a reprieve?" I inquired.

"Oh yeah," she answered.

"Who was all there?" I asked.

"Well, there were Jim's two brothers' families which meant we had four kids under the age of three running around, and they all had runny noses."

"I thought you said you weren't going if any of the kids were sick?"

"Yeah, well no one told me the kids were sick. Oh Dad, it was so gross. There was snot hanging out constantly from their noses the whole time. Suzy sneezed one time and all this snot came flying out and hanging from her nose and chin. I thought I was going to throw up."

I laughed.

"I guess when it's your own kids, it's different," I said.

Although I can't honestly say I agree with that. When the kids were little and had a runny nose, Linda, who has an internal fortitude of iron, had this squeeze bulb kind of thing that she would use to suck out the snot when they were congested. It got to the point that whenever the kids saw that thing appear, *whoosh*, they were gone. I tried not to be in the same room when she finally found them in their hiding spot.

"And there was even a grosser part," she continued. "Jim's middle brother was holding his eight month old son in the rocking chair after dinner, and the baby threw up everywhere. It went all over the left side of this face and neck, and it slowly dripped down onto his chest. The bad part was that the baby had some peas for dinner, and the puke was all green and slimy. I started to retch. I had to leave the room."

By then, I was really laughing.

"Gosh Elizabeth, what are you going to do when it's your own and they do that?" I managed to get out.

"I don't know", she moaned.

"I guess you're going to be doing a lot of retching and throwing up in the beginning, huh?"

"Oh, I hope not. I'm not sure I can take it. You know the other thing that Jim and I noticed was the noise level. There were three kids under the age of three running around screaming and yelling on a hard-wood floor. The noise just echoed off the walls and floor. Boy, it sure is something that you have to get used to."

"I know," I said. "Your mother and I say the same thing after we've had company or people at the house. It seems to go from all noise to all quiet, and you really don't notice it until you have the opposite happen. Now you know why your grandfather always kept asking us when we were leaving when you and your brother were little."

She giggled. "Yeah, I know now."

I heard the hair dryer upstairs.

"It sounds like your mother is just about done. I can hear the hair dryer."

I made my way up the stairs to the master bedroom. I always try to make a noisy entrance so I don't startle Linda and she accuses me of sneaking up on her...again.

"Hey, your daughter is on the phone," I called out as I entered the bedroom doorway.

The dryer stopped.

"Tell her I'm busy," came her short reply.

"Hey, I heard that!" came Elizabeth's retort from the speaker.

My wife smiled as I handed her the cell phone.

"Would I do that to my baby girl?" she cooed into the phone.

I just walked out shaking my head.

* * *

Linda's cell phone rang around noon on Sunday. It was Elizabeth.

"Hey Dad, can you look to see if you have the title to my car?" she asked. "I'll need it when we trade in my car."

"I'm thinking we don't have it. I'm pretty sure that your mother gave that to you when your car was paid off," I said back.

"Yeah, I know. I'm pretty sure she did. I'm also pretty sure it probably got shuffled around during the move and ended up getting thrown out."

After Elizabeth was married, one of the first things Linda and I suggested to her was to get her car re-registered in her and Jim's name. When we bought the car, my name had to be on the title since I was the co-signor. When the car was finally paid off and the title arrived, we handed it to her with that suggestion. Actually we suggested a lot of things to do for names and re-registering of things after she was married, but it looks like they were overcome by new married life.

"I'll look, but I'm not holding our much hope for it."

In our bedroom closet is a small, gray fire-proof, water-proof safe. It contains all the important family documents like birth certificates, social security cards, our will, and other legal papers. We purchased it after Linda's father passed away a couple of years ago. Her mother did a pretty good job of keeping the important papers together along with construction dates of home improvements, purchase dates of appliances, and other important information, but in the several years since her passing, some of the documents got scattered or lost. We didn't want that to happen to us.

I searched through the contents of the safe envelope by envelope hoping to come across the car title. When I had reached the back of the container, it confirmed what I had already suspected. Linda had also gone through an old container we used to use for important papers years ago thinking she may have stuck it in there by mistake. No luck.

I had to leave for the airport soon, so I went upstairs to take a shower, and Linda called Elizabeth back with the bad news. While

I was still in the shower, Linda stood in the doorway and told me about the conversation she had with my daughter. See, when she's bad, she's *my daughter.*

"Elizabeth needs to calm down," Linda started. "She's all stressed out about buying this car and not having the title to hers."

My wife is the calm one in these situations.

"It's ok, she'll get through it," I replied.

"I know. Now she's saying that we have to complete some on-line form for the state, and have it notarized to get a new title. I told her she needed to chill out and see if the dealership where they are buying the car can help them."

See, I told you Linda was the calm one.

"Good idea," I mumbled, water streaming in my face.

"Did she say anything to you about it?"

"No, she just asked me to look for the title."

"Oh, so I'm the one that has to take the take the brunt. You can call her next time."

Oh boy.

Linda had picked me up from the airport on the following Friday after I arrived back in Pittsburgh from my every other week business trip, and we were on our way home when her cell phone rang. I grabbed the phone and answered it. It was Elizabeth.

"Hello Chloe," I said sweetly into the phone.

"Hey Dad, what are you doing back so soon? Don't you normally come in after eight?"

"Yeah, but for some reason, the airline switched the times of my regular flight and got me back now. It sure is good to head back home while it's still daylight in December. What's going on?"

"I called to vent."

Oh geez.

"Vent about what?" I asked.

"About this stupid car. You know, this sales guy at the dealership is not doing his job," she started.

"What do you mean?" I jumped in.

"First of all, he told us that there were several vehicles in the area exactly like the one we wanted. That was last Saturday. We haven't heard from all week."

"Maybe he's still looking for the best deal," I interjected.

"No, that's not it," came Elizabeth's quick reply. "I messaged him yesterday and asked for an update. He sent back that he was still negotiating with another dealership in the area for the one car he found. He then asked if he couldn't get that color, what would be our second color choice."

"Well, that doesn't sound too bad," I said.

"I didn't think so either, until I talked it over with Jim. He wants the silver color and nothing else."

"And what if the sales guy can't find a silver color like the one you want?"

"Jim said that we would go somewhere else to buy the car. This is going to take forever!"

"It doesn't sound like the sales guy is working too hard for his commission," I said back to her.

"Oh no, the on-line guy doesn't work by commission. He's salary, so there's no reason for him to be in a big hurry."

"Not necessarily," I replied. "A disgruntled customer is a disgruntled customer no matter what the reason is. If he doesn't produce, then his job is in jeopardy."

"Well, I sent him a message that if I didn't get an update by noon today, I would take my business else where."

"Elizabeth, you need to calm down. What does Jim think about all this?"

"That's another thing. He's not upset at all, and that makes me even more upset!"

Oh boy.

"So let me make sure I understand. You're upset that you don't have a car yet, and that the salesman is not keeping you updated, and you're upset because Jim isn't upset?" I repeated.

Silence on the other end.

"Well....yeah."

I sat up in the car seat.

"Are you sure?"

"I know it sounds funny, but that's the way I feel right now. Remember, I am pregnant."

A giggle from the phone.

"Alright, why don't you just cool down, and see what happens over the weekend. If nothing, then you have every right to be upset and go somewhere else. Agree?"

"Yeah, you're right. It's just that Jim is so laid back," her voice trailed off.

"I know. Call next week if nothing happens, ok?"

"Ok, bye."

I closed the phone and looked at Linda.

"Was that your daughter venting?" she asked.

See, again with *your daughter*.

I let out a deep breath.

"Yes, it seems as though the world is not running on Elizabeth time, and she's upset about it. The salesman at the dealership is not keeping her up to date, so she sent him a scathing message that he better get her a car or else."

Linda shook her head.

"See, she's just like you. She locks onto something and just won't let go until it's done."

"Well, that's not necessarily a bad thing, is it? I did that when I first met you at college," I countered.

She laughed. "You silver-tongued devil."

I leaned back in the seat and put my hands behind my head. Oh yeah.

* * *

When Elizabeth found out she was going to have a baby, one of the first things she did was make sure Jim knew that he was now the man to clean out the litter box each day. Never having a cat, Jim balked at the suggestion of doing such a lowly, gross thing.

Elizabeth warned him that there is a parasite linked with litter boxes that can be dangerous to pregnant women. It's called toxoplasmosis. I remember my mother telling me about that when Linda was pregnant with Elizabeth.

He couldn't withstand her onslaught. The continual verbal barrage was too much. Jim relented and agreed to clean the litter box each day. It was hilarious to hear Elizabeth tell the first time Jim cleaned the litter box.

"I was sitting on the couch watching television," she began. "Jim announced he was going into the abyss to clean the litter box."

The litter box is actually in a small closet off the living room with a cat door and a little light that comes on when it detects motion. Sure don't want Chloe being scared in the dark, or in this case, Jim.

"Jim came into the room with this getup. He is dressed in a long sleeved, flannel shirt, safety glasses, a bandanna covering his nose and mouth, and bright green rubber gloves on his hands. He looked hysterical. I didn't know if he was going to rob a bank or perform surgery," Elizabeth explained.

"He slowly opened the closet door, and shut it behind him. I turned down the tv so I could listen. I heard him start to scrape the sifter through the litter, and I heard "Oh God, this is so gross." I'm rolling on the couch laughing but trying to keep quiet. More scraping, more "this is so gross" moans, and a couple of gags as well."

"Chloe was standing outside the closet looking through the translucent pet door watching Jim, her ears twitched each time Jim moaned and complained. Finally Jim emerged from the closet with his found treasure wrapped up in a plastic grocery bag and tossed it into the trash can in the garage."

"He's all sweaty, and looks like he just came in from working outside. I'm watching him all the while trying to keep a straight face. He plops down in the chair, looking completely drained."

"That is so gross," Jim said. "I don't know how you do that each day. I almost puked."

"Don't worry honey," she replied. "After a couple of weeks, it will be just another thing."

"Yeah, right," was all he could muster.

"What are you going to do when you have to change the baby?"

"I'm not sure, but I'll probably wait for you to get home," he said flipping through the tv channels. "Maybe I'll just call Mom. She can be here in a few minutes.

"Oh no, mister. None of that for our child," came Elizabeth's reply. "Mom told me a story or two of my dad doing that to me when I was little."

Hey wait, how did I get involved in this conversation?

§ Chapter 4

Man-Thoughts On Pregnancy

This pregnancy with my daughter is somewhat surreal. I never really thought about it during all those years she was growing up. Ok, well, I did think about it, but mostly from a how to prevent it perspective. It was our good fortune that she was a really down-to-earth, sensible, intelligent person. She dated some in high school, but never really had a boyfriend. She had more of a herd mentality...a group of them would do things rather than going out on a date.

She did have one guy that she hung out with for a period of time. He was not what I would call someone that you would bring home to meet Mom. He had really long hair, and a bunch of ear rings, and he smoked. Smoking was one of Elizabeth's taboos, so I was surprised that she saw him more than once. I did mention to her one time that she shouldn't date anyone who had more ear rings than she did. It wasn't long before he was history. I don't think it took much of a push to get that accomplished.

She met Jim while working a summer job as a cashier at a local supermarket. They are the same age, but with Jim's birthday falling when it did, he was actually a year behind her in high school. She was a sophomore in college when they met. Jim had never really dated in high school either, but their relationship blossomed over the summer and on into the following school year.

Jim is a good man. He is the youngest of three boys. He has good values and morals, and is very good with money; something that Elizabeth needs to be reined in from time to time. He has a good job with the county in their computer technology department and is doing well. He's all you could ask for in a son-in-law.

It's also amazing that Elizabeth is actually pregnant. For years when she was younger, she was dead set against being pregnant and having a baby, and made her opinions known many times. I remember our short conversation about those weeks ago.

"You know Elizabeth, all those years when you were little, you said you weren't going to have a baby. You wanted to adopt."

"Geez Dad, what was I, like three of four years old?"

A video began to play in my mind.

I came home from work one day in early spring. We lived in Jacksonville, North Carolina where I was stationed in the service. It was a beautiful, sunny day. Elizabeth was probably three of four years old, and as usual, came running to me as I came in the door. I scooped her up in my arms and gave her a big kiss.

"Hi Daddy. I have a 'agina."

I'm sure a look of shock came across my face.

"What did you say, baby?"

"I have a 'agina."

Just then, Linda poked her head around the corner down the hallway.

"What is she saying?" I asked.

"She's telling you she has a vagina."

I was stunned. I looked at my blonde haired, blue-eyed little princess.

"And how did that subject come up?" I managed to ask after a short pause.

"Katy was over this morning and we got to talking about babies," replied my wife.

Katy lived across the street from us. She was married to a Marine helicopter pilot, and had two boys that were in junior high school. Katy was a lot of fun, and you never knew what might come out of her mouth next. Her husband was somewhat of a celebrity since he had been one of the pilots for the President's helicopter.

"But how did this subject come up?"

"Elizabeth asked where babies come from, so we told her. What did you want me to say, the stork brings them?"

Well...no," I stammered. "But geez..."

"Daddy, I don't want to have babies," interrupted Elizabeth. "I want to adopt one."

"Oh really? That's good."

"Yeah," she said softly while she played with the collar of my uniform. "I don't want one coming out my 'agina."

Oh God.

* * *

It's funny how random thoughts or questions pop up when you least expect it about your kids, and especially the pregnant ones. One evening, Linda and I were sitting in front of the tv watching a football game. Ok, I was watching the game and she was doing a word search puzzle. A thought hit me.

"Do you think Elizabeth is ready to be a mother?"

She looked up from her book. "What do you mean?"

"Well, I remember when you were pregnant with Elizabeth, being a mother seemed to be the most natural thing in the world for you. I'm not getting that same feeling with Elizabeth."

She thought for a moment.

"I have to be honest, I have some reservations too. I guess what concerns me is her fear of holding little babies. When we went out to Jim's brother's house just after they had their little boy, she wanted nothing to do with holding the baby."

"I guess it's different when it's your own," I said back.

"Let's hope so, you know?" Linda replied. "It's not like they come with instructions."

Boy, don't I know that.

As the time grows nearer for the baby to arrive, I've come to notice a small, nagging issue in the back of my mind. It never really jumps out ands says 'here I am, deal with me.' No, it's more like a ghost or apparition that slowly appears and then slowly fades away. Since Elizabeth has been married, the thought of being a grandfather has passed through my mind once or twice. I watched people I work with, or friends, become grandparents, and it seemed to always be the other guy. Now I'm staring down the barrel of the gun pointed at me.

Don't get me wrong. Being a grandfather is the normal course of things, sort of like the circle of life you read about. My children have grown into adults and are now taking the next step forward. It's my turn to do so as well. But I remember grandparents as being old, and retired. I don't consider myself old, although I'm older than my parents were when they first became grandparents to Elizabeth. And I'm definitely not retired.

I look at my wife and just know she'll be a wonderful grandmother because she was a wonderful mother. She knows just the right way to take care of "owies", or wipe away tears, or knows how to pick the right Christmas present. My son will be a terrific uncle, and my mother and siblings will treat the baby like gold.

I look back at my own memories of grandfathers, but unfortunately there's not much to remember. Both of my grandfathers died by the time I was seven. I do have a fuzzy, faded memory of both.

The grandfather on my Dad's side was a great hunter, fisherman, and trapper. He loved the outdoors and spent a lot of his time there. I remember being in an outbuilding near his house with my Dad when I was probably four or five years old. It was late spring because the weather felt like it was getting warmer. My grandfather was standing in the middle of the darkened room, an animal carcass was hanging by the tail on a wire, and he was skinning the fur off of it with his big knife. I remember not being scared, but more intrigued at what he was doing. When I became of age, I also hunted, fished, and trapped, and that memory would come back to me from time to time as I was skinning an animal.

The memory of my Mom's father is even more faded. He died unexpectedly when I was three or four years old. I do have one memory of him standing in a small garden near tomato plants that were staked up in the back yard of his house. We lived in the country, and my grandparents lived maybe a hundred and fifty yards from my parents' house. I remember the dirt being a dark brown, and the plants were a bright green as the warm sunshine reflected off them. I remember watching my grandfather working on one of the plants and, then all of a sudden, everything went black. The only thing I remember after that is being tossed around in all my clothes while wearing a bulky jacket. That's the end of the memory.

Years later, my mother's only brother, Uncle Don, told me that I had stepped off the bank of the creek that ran behind both of our houses and fell into the water. For a few seconds, I guess no one missed me. It was my uncle, who was fourteen at the time, finally realized where I was and jumped into the water and fished me out.

That about summarizes my grandfather memories. I do

have a lifetime of wonderful memories of my two grandmothers though. They were completely opposite of each other, but they treated me great. My Dad's mother loved to laugh, smoke, and drink beer. She possessed a raucous laugh, and loved a good time. My Mom's mother, on the other hand, loved to draw, sing, and sew. I'm not sure alcohol ever passed between her lips her entire life. She lived with us in my parents' house for over thirty years after my grandfather passed (minus a few years with husband number two) until her death at age eighty-nine. She was a quiet, sensitive woman.

My kids have had the good fortune of having both sets of grandparents for most of their young lives. For the longest time, they were the only grandkids on either side of the family, and were spoiled rotten by everyone. Both were well into their teens before the first grandparent, who happened to be my father, passed away. I know they have good memories of all of them because whenever we get together, we inevitably start talking about funny events that happened when they were young, and grandparents always seem to make it into the stories.

I can now look back at how my father and father-in-law treated my kids as great examples. I only hope that I can do their memories justice.

* * *

I was traveling on business again this week and with the Christmas holiday just a couple of weeks away, most of my focus was ensuring we were ready as a company to take advantage of any last minute shipments. I didn't hear anything from Elizabeth, not a rare thing, but there were two somewhat bigger things that Linda worked through this past week.

When traveling, I always call Linda from my mid-point airport, and the final destination airport just to check in. I called from the mid-point airport as I always do, and Linda proceeded to tell me that she had just spoken with the realtor and had gotten an offer on her parents' house. Of course, the timing was just wonderful because I had just left for the week. It was a cash settlement, which was the best type of offer, but the buyer wanted to be in the house in a week. It was a divorced man and his two teen-aged children, and they wanted to be in the house before the

Christmas holiday.

The good part – the house had been sitting empty for almost two years, and it was showing signs of wear. A house is like a car, if you don't run it and keep up with the maintenance, it will start to fall apart. We all did the best we could of trying to maintain it and take care of it, but with the fast pace of our lifestyle, kids' activities, and not to mention that Linda and I are two and a half hours away, this offer was a good thing.

The bad part, or should I say, sad part - this closed the final chapter on my in-laws. My in-laws lived in that house for fifty-five years, and it represented many great memories for a lot of people. It was the center point for all the holiday celebrations, funeral wakes, wedding parties, family reunions, summer cookouts, and general get-togethers. My father-in-law had the biggest garden in town, and was famous for his tomatoes. It seemed that the garden got just a little bigger each year as more and more of the yard fell victim to the blades of his roto-tiller.

After a lot of discussion and soul-searching, my wife and her brother decided to take the offer on the house. The buyer was very excited to get into the house, and it looked like he would take good care of it.

Once that decision was made, plans were put into place to get the final furniture and other odds and ends from the house. It took us a full two days of working from sunrise to sunset of getting everything that was left out of the house. We thought we had done a good job in the spring when we cleared out two large dumpsters of items, but the basement and garage held more things than you could believe. Who needs five hand saws of the exact same type?

It was a tough situation for my wife and her brother when we locked the door and pulled it closed for the very last time on that cold and snowy Sunday evening, knowing that they would never live there again. There were tears, and questions about 'doing the right thing', but in the end, we bid each other good bye and went our separate ways. It was a long, quiet ride home.

On a happier note this past week, Linda got into the diaper mode. Elizabeth told her that she wanted to use cloth diapers for the baby which translates to more expensive, at least in the beginning. She wanted to be a 'green' mother. Elizabeth has always been this way. When she was in fourth or fifth grade, she had an environmental class, and has been on her environmental soap box ever since. She required that we (actually me) install low pressure shower heads, place a brick in each of the toilet tanks to reduce water usage, and use only natural cleaning products, nothing with man-made chemicals. Looking back on it now, I guess it wasn't so bad.

Anyway, Elizabeth complained that there were no 'diaper places' around Harrisburg like the one she found online, but guess what? There was one near us. So Linda looked it up and found that it was actually about twenty minutes from our house. To get into this store, she had to make an appointment, and take a class on cloth diapers. I mean, how hard can it be to use cloth diapers?

Two hours (and $124) later, she returned to the house, laid everything out on the table, and started to explain to me how it all worked.

Now wait. We used cloth diapers with Elizabeth, you know, the white ones that had the small blue "Curity' stamp in the corner of each diaper. You folded it up, fastened it with pins on each side, and put on the plastic pants. Waaalah, done.

Oh no, not now. There are special materials that the cloth diapers are made out of so they can breathe, but not leak (read costs more money). They even make diapers out of bamboo at a cost of eighteen dollars a pop. Oh yeah, it gets better. They make 'all in one' diapers where the diaper has a pocket that you slip in another cloth diaper and fasten it with Velcro strips. And they make these little tabs that go over the Velcro strips so they don't wear out in the wash.

Remember the old, smelly diaper pail? No more. There's this type of cloth bag that you can put the dirty diaper in and it won't smell or leak. There are also special cloth wipes that are guaranteed to work better than the store bought brands.

And last, but not least, it all has to be washed in a special, natural detergent.

Boy, I'm in the wrong business.

*   *   *

As usual, the dawning of the New Year came and went while I was sound asleep. I've never been one for ringing in the New Year with all the pageantry and silliness that is associated with it. When I was younger, I was known to have hoisted an adult beverage or two in celebration, but in 2009, I was in bed by 10 pm and slept the night soundly, although I think I did hear some fireworks in the neighborhood around midnight.

Linda, however, is the night owl, and couldn't let it pass without her being part of it even in some small way. About11:30, she got out of bed and headed downstairs to watch one of the tv programs to help usher in 2010. I was totally oblivious to it.

When I woke up that morning, one of my first thoughts was that this is going to be a year of big change for us. We will have a stranger arriving into our midst soon, someone who we have never met before, or seen before, but who will be loved dearly from the first second. Lots of preparation has been going on for this person's appearance, and there is yet much to do.

Linda's and my lives will change somewhat, but the lives of Elizabeth and Jim will be changed forever. It happens like that with your first-born. All the new things you and your wife learn and have to deal with as new parents.

Probably the most difficult thing I remember is the fatigue and exhaustion from the feedings every couple of hours all day and all night. Both of our children were bottle-fed, so it wasn't really a big deal whether Elizabeth or I got up for the feeding. However, I was accused of faking being asleep when either one of the kids cried at night. What can I say, I'm a heavy sleeper.

Elizabeth is getting set up to breast feed. She's taken classes, and talked with her cousin who is currently breast-feeding to get some advice on how to do it correctly. I've overheard conversations about three hundred dollar breast pumps, maternity bras, and the term 'nipple confusion.' I'm not sure what all goes into getting ready to do it, or what it takes to complete it, and to tell you the truth, I'd like to remain somewhat ignorant in this area.

Linda has a free pass onto the internet now that the baby's arrival is getting nearer. It seems that the majority of the time when I call her while I'm traveling, she's says that she's on the computer 'looking' for things for the baby. I'm not exactly sure, but it's probably more 'buying' than it is 'looking.'

Over the holidays, Linda and I took our share of ribbing from my brothers about becoming grandparents in the near future. Lots of jokes about memory loss, each of us needing a cane, and eating at four in the afternoon and then going right to bed were tossed about. The tough thing is that my hair has been getting a little thinner, ok, a lot thinner, and I certainly heard about that as well. It seemed as if no subject was off-limits during the holiday. I have to admit though, it was a good time.

It had been several days since we heard from Elizabeth, but that's not real unusual. If they're busy, or have classes to go to for the baby, the number of calls decreases. Linda and I were getting ready to drive to Pittsburgh and celebrate Ryan's birthday with him when her cell phone rang. I could tell it was Elizabeth on the other end just by the way she answered the phone. Knowing that these conversations take a while, I headed upstairs to take a shower.

We were in the car heading to Pittsburgh when I asked Linda about her conversation with Elizabeth.

"Oh, she just wanted to tell us about her latest doctor's appointment and how it went."

"And how did it go?" I asked.

"I guess it went well. The doctor said that she's gaining the right amount of weight between visits, but if you listen to Elizabeth, she looks like an aircraft carrier," she replied.

"How much does she weigh now?"

"I don't know, I didn't ask her. Didn't sound like a question to ask this time around. The doctor did say she looks like she's at week thirty-one and a half. Remember last time, he said she looked like she was a little ahead of schedule? Well, it must have been the way the baby was laying because he dropped her back a week or so."

"I still think they should give you a due week, ya know?" I said.

"And by the way, she also mentioned that she doesn't want the bumper pads for the crib. She just read an article about how babies have gotten their heads caught between the pad and the crib and have smothered. Now she wants some plastic balloon kind of thing that you tie onto each individual slat on the crib."

"You mean like something that they use for boats tying up at the dock to keep them from bumping it?"

"Yeah, I guess something like that. I haven't seen them. Ready for this? They cost $219 for the set."

"Wow, the price just keeps going up on this crib."

"Elizabeth did say that Wednesday's are going to be long now. She said they have a baby class from seven to nine pm for the next six weeks."

"Geez, they have more classes for this baby than you and I did for both kids."

"Well honey, it's a different time. Actually I think it's great that they have all this information to give to new parents. I wished we would have had that."

"Oh yeah, I know. I agree, I think its good too," I said.

A small pause.

"Just think, our daughter is going to have a baby. They look so young to have kids. But we were what, six or seven years younger than them when we had Elizabeth. I'm sure people thought you were still in high school," I said.

Another pause.

"Come to think of it, you were only two years out of high school. Wow, we were young. But I have no regrets. We bundled her up and away we'd go. Remember how she used to ride in her seat on the back of your bike?" I added.

One of the great things about being in the military is staying in shape; one of the bad things about being in the military is staying in shape. As an officer, you have to do a lot of running on your own to ensure that you can lead your troops during physical training.

When we were at the base in North Carolina, one of the Sunday activities that Linda and I enjoyed was running and biking. We actually started it when Linda was pregnant with Elizabeth. She was nearing her due date and the doctor said that things weren't moving along as well as he'd liked, so it would be good for Linda would do some walking. We would wind around the streets of our subdivision. It was a beautiful area to be out and about with the tall loblolly pines and the beautiful magnolia trees with the warm (sometimes hot) sunshine. When Elizabeth came long, I would run my normal three mile course, and Linda would push her in the stroller for a distance and then we'd meet back at the house. When Elizabeth was old enough, we bought a child's seat to attach to Linda's bike, and a little pink helmet for her, and we'd all go together.

I can still remember Linda riding in front of me on the bike as I ran, and Elizabeth was sitting in the seat right behind her sucking on her thumb (she was big thumb sucker). Each time that Linda would push on one of the pedals, Elizabeth's head would bob to that side. It was almost hypnotizing watching Elizabeth's head bob back and forth with each push.

"You know, even though we lived near Harrisburg for fourteen years," Linda said breaking my thoughts, "I'm not sure I remember how to get to the hospital."

"Oh, it will come back to you, "I replied.

"Yeah, I think once I get back there and see familiar things, it'll come back to me."

"Besides," I continued, "we have the gps just in case your memory isn't what it used to be," I said with a wink.

A typical response...a punch in the shoulder.

Elizabeth's baby shower is now just a few days away, but with my astute powers of observation, I would know something is going on even if I was unaware of that. Little things have been appearing in the house for Linda's trip across the state. Munchy things. Little fish crackers, small packages of cookies, and the always-have-to-have licorice bits for the long trip. Linda has always been a snacky type of traveler. She always stashes a bag of munchy items in the car before we leave, and then we pretty much graze during the whole trip. I would like to say that it actually saves money, but I'm not sure at this point because we always seem to stop and get something else anyway.

She's planning on leaving Friday and staying through Monday which means I'll be batcheloring it for a couple of days before I fly out. Had I not had such an early flight, we'd go together and drive back home on Sunday so I could leave on my flight. Still, it works out this way as well because now she can stay a couple of extra days to help Elizabeth around the house with things. Linda said that when she told Elizabeth that she would stay a day or two longer, the first thing Elizabeth asked about was putting up the crib.

One of the things that Linda has wanted to do is to go shopping for the baby, just the two of us. Well, I got my first taste of shopping for a newborn last night, sort of like a baptism by fire. Linda had ordered those rubber balloon-type of bumper pads, and then received an e-mail message yesterday from the company that they would not be shipped for another week. This put her into a panic because now she had nothing to give Elizabeth at the baby shower in a few days. After several anxious minutes, she came up with the idea that she could run over to one of the chain baby stores and pick up a few things that were still left on Elizabeth's list and give those to her at the shower. I said that I would like to go with her and share in the experience of shopping for the baby. Yeah, right.

We left after supper and drove the twenty-five minutes to the mall where the baby store is located. It was pretty cold out, so I had the heater running full blast as we drove. Once it got warm in the car, Linda sat back in the seat and was quiet for the most of the ride. When I asked if she was tired, she said that she just chillin'.

If you've ever wanted to watch the dead come back to life, you should have been with me when Linda and I entered the baby store. Linda was walking slowly across the parking lot to the door, limping a little, and complained that her leg hurt from doing her workout routine earlier in the day. The minute we walked through the front door of the store, Linda's excitement level skyrocketed. You could actually see the energy level peak. She was in her element. Nothing else in the world mattered. As we walked through the door, she started squealing and pointing for me to look at this, or look at that.

"Oh look at the pajamas with the little feet. Aren't they cute?"

"Yep, very cute."

"Oh, look at these with the little duckies on it. Aren't they just precious?"

"Duckies, I just love them," I answered, rolling my eyes.

"I'm going to have so much fun shopping for our grandchild," she squealed as she shook my arm.

"Yeah, somehow I didn't think there would be a real problem."

I have to be honest, this was the first time I had been in a large store for babies. It was pretty much how I had imagined, at least to a point. My first realization was that babies are big business. There are things of every conceivable notion in the store. We looked at diapers, some were even organic, some were made from bamboo, and some were just how I remembered them...plain and white. We looked at crib sheets, and most were just like the diapers we looked at. Some were organic, and some were just in the package. Just imagine all the different things under the sun you can have for a baby and that's what it seemed to me.

I did get a chance to look at the crib where my $640 went.

It looked pretty nice until I read the fine print. The bold print said that it was a cherry finish, but the fine print said that it was fiber board covered with cherry veneer. For that price, it should be solid cherry wood. Having done some wood-working before, I know the value of good wood. No worries though. The thought is much more important than the price.

While we were wandering around the store looking for diapers, I made a turn with the cart down an aisle where I probably shouldn't have been, at least in my mind. Yes, it was the aisle with all the breast-feeding items. I don't know why I'm so skittish about that, but it just seems to hit me in a bad place. While we were standing there in the aisle, Linda had stopped (on purpose I think) to look at something, she asked me a question.

"Elizabeth asked me this past week if I thought you would be uncomfortable if she was nursing in front of you."

"What did you tell her?"

"I said yes, you would be uncomfortable."

"Yep, you would be right."

My memory took me back to a somewhat embarrassing situation when I was in college. There was a gang of five or six college kids I ran around with at home during the summers off from school. We all attended the same church and played on the church softball team. Two members of the group were a married couple who were just a few years older than us and had been out in the working world. We usually ended up at their house after the games for pizza, or just to visit at times.

It just so happened that during one summer they had their first baby. Since my parents lived less than a mile away, I would stop in once or twice during the week to see if Terri or Kevin needed any help. Kevin worked all day, and had a fairly big yard, so I would cut the grass for them, or do errands.

It was a bright June afternoon when I pulled into their driveway. I knocked on the screen door, and Terri said to come in. I walked through the door into the living room. Terri was sitting on the sofa that faced the front door and she was nursing the baby.

"Whoa!" I said putting my hands up, slamming on the brakes, and backing out of the doorway. "I didn't know you were doing that," I stammered.

"It's ok, come on in," Terri said.

I hesitated, but slowly made my way into the house and

kept my eyes glued to the floor. I felt for the chair near the doorway and sat down not daring to look up.

"Does this bother you?" she asked.

"Well, um...yeah, but...it's just that..."

"Look, I know some people get embarrassed. I'll cover up."

I heard fabric moving.

"There. All covered up. Better?"

I looked up hesitantly. She was sitting there with a yellow blanket covering her whole upper body. It covered everything, but I still knew what was going on underneath that blanket. I couldn't get past it.

"Hey Terri, um, how about if I come back later and see if you or Kevin need anything?"

"Ok, that will be fine," she softly replied.

I dashed out the door and made a beeline straight for my car.

As I think more about it now, I guess I look at nursing a baby as an intimate time between mother and baby, and no one else should be involved. It's certainly not a group activity. Maybe the father, but definitely no one else. Call me old-fashioned, but that's my story and I'm sticking to it.

Anyway, I got more information in that aisle than I ever wanted. Linda pointed out to me the different type of breast pumps, from the $30 manual pumps to the $200 do-it-yourself pumps. I saw salve for cracked nipples, plastic covers for sore nipples, and gauze covers for leaking nipples. More than I wanted to know. I know it's just a fact of life, but it was time for me to leave. Linda gave me the list and put me in charge of toy selection.

"So it's ok if I pick up footballs, baseballs, and few bats?" I asked innocently, trying to regain my masculinity.

"That's good if it's a boy. What if it's a girl?"

"Hey, I can still pick up footballs and baseballs. Look at Elizabeth. She could hit a baseball better than most of the boys on her Little League team, and threw a football better than the boys in the neighborhood."

I never let Elizabeth being a girl diminish her options of what she could and couldn't play. When she was old enough to hold a bat, she and I would go out into the back yard and I would toss a little plastic ball to her, or toss a small nerf football back and forth for hours.

"I would say she could hit better than all of the boys on the team. I think that's why she didn't get along very well with them," replied Linda.

I wandered over to the infant toy section and began my search for just the right toy for my first grandchild. I glanced at the list and compared it to what I saw on the shelf. The first thing I was able to find was a bird called "Jacques Peacock." Oh geez, who comes up with these names? It was a small, colorful bird made of a felt-type material that actually sounded like it was filled with buckwheat when you shook it. It had a few things that made sounds and rotated on it. I examined it closely. No, it just didn't do it for me, too feminine, I continued my search. Next, I found a farmyard ball with pictures of different animals on it. Now this was more like it. I threw it around for a little bit, and decided it would do, so I tossed it into the cart.

I couldn't find anymore toys that I thought were cool enough for my grandchild, so I headed back to find Linda. She was over at the crib sheets area looking for a few things on the list. After finding one more item, we decided that we had enough and went to check out. Although the total came to just a little less than $85, I didn't think it was that bad considering all the items we bought.

I also finally got to look at one of those "snappy" things that take the place of diaper safety pins. Think of a T-shaped item made of plastic with the stem of the T made very short. The three ends are wide with protruding small plastic teeth that I guess bite into the cloth diaper. It was pretty flexible and stretchy, but I didn't pull on it too hard because I was afraid it would break, and then all hell would break loose from you know who. At five dollars a piece, just a little tug sufficed.

After we got back to the house and unloaded the packages, Linda and I sat down to relax for just a bit before we headed upstairs to get ready for bed. As usual, Linda was doing one of her word puzzles and I was hunting around the television stations for anything half decent to watch. I turned to Linda.

"Do you think Elizabeth is ready for this birthing thing? I mean, you can read only so much about it."

Linda put down her book. "I think so. She and I have talked about it. I tried to tell her what to expect."

"Is she scared or anything like that?"

"No, she's not scared."

"You know what?" I said. "I didn't think she would be."

When Linda was taking me to the airport today, a thought crossed my mind that the baby is almost here, and soon to become a reality. Up until just a few weeks ago when I saw Elizabeth and her belly, the baby was a dream. It's just about five weeks and counting if the due date is anywhere near correct. A new life into the big world, our world.

If the baby could hear me now and understand what I was saying, I would tell it that we are all anxiously waiting for his or her appearance (It's a general belief among the family that your parents know what they're having, they're just being very secretive about it.) By the way, all of the preparations are ready.

The crib is set up and stocked full of toys. The changing table is next to the crib for all those mother and child bonding times. I'm trying to envision what that will look like the first few times. I think it will be somewhat comical at first as I see it in my mind's eye. Your mother was retching when a couple of little kids were running around with snotty noses. What will it be like when she changes your diaper for the first time and sees what presents you have left for her? I'm thinking that Dad's time at the changing table will be even more limited. He was retching when cleaning out the cat litter box. Oh yes new baby, your parents aren't the greatest yet at navigating brutal odors and toxic baby substances, but they will be. All new parents eventually do. I'm not so sure about your great grandfather though. My mother told me stories of him tying a clean diaper around his nose and mouth like they did in the old cowboy movies when he changed diapers. He fought in the Korean war and took a big piece of shrapnel in his leg, but a dirty diaper kicked his butt. Oh, and one other thing. Don't forget to ask your mother about all the times she would run around the house naked when we tried to get her to change a diaper or get into the bath tub. She'd just squeal and laugh and we'd chase her and pinch her little butt. See how she explains that one to you.

The car seat is in the car and will be checked by the police department this week to make sure that it's installed correctly. I'm glad that your parents are doing that now instead of the waiting to pick you up at the hospital like your grandmother and I did with your mother.

The diapers were lovingly washed in a special detergent to

make them ultra soft, neatly folded, and then stacked in your room waiting to be used. Your mother doesn't think that she has enough. I mean thirty-six diapers. Come on, how many will you use in the first week? Your grandmother tells me you'll use a lot and that we'll have to get some more for you and her. Your mother is trying to be kind to the environment and using cloth diapers so she won't add to the filling of the landfills with plastics that will take hundreds of years to decay. I have to tell you that she has always been this way. You can learn a lot from her on this subject.

All the breastfeeding equipment is purchased and ready to use to make sure you get the best in feedings and nourishment that mankind and technology can offer. I have to say that I'm a little uneasy talking about this subject for some reason. My mother didn't breastfeed me, and your grandmother didn't breastfeed your mother, so I have no first-hand experience at this. Everything that I know is from either reading about it or listening to conversations. I must say that I was on the verge of leaving some of the conversations because I was uncomfortable. I hope you don't get "nipple confusion" because from what I've overheard, that's a tough one. I've always tried to be a helper and supporter of my family, but I'm sorry to say that you and your mother will have to work this one out on your own. Don't worry about it though, she has a nursing coach, so my bet is that you'll be fine.

Your names have been selected by your parents, but yet again, they won't tell anyone what they are. Your soon to be father said to your grandmother that she will be somewhat surprised at the names they have chosen. Hmmm, I wonder what that means. Your grandmother and I had dinner last night with your great-grandmother and she thinks that your mother knows what she's having. I told her that if she does know what she's having, she's playing it very cool because she hasn't let on one bit that she knows. I myself don't think she knows because I know my daughter.

Your soon-to-be-mother has already started to pack her bag for the hospital stay when you decide it's time to make your appearance into the world. They have been taking classes on what to do, where to go, and who to see. You already have your first doctor's visit scheduled. They won't allow you out of the hospital until that was done. Your soon-to-be grandmother has started to talk about what she will need to pack when she makes the four hour trip after she gets "the call" from her daughter.

Your mother has done everything humanly possible to take care of herself, and in essence, take care of you before you were born. She has taken her vitamins religiously everyday. She has only eaten those foods that were the best for you and her. She always checked the packages of everything she cooked and ate to make sure they did not contain any harmful ingredients. Once, when she thought she had eaten some food with alcohol in it, she excused herself from the table where several friends were eating, went upstairs, and forced herself to throw up. She did not want any of that alcohol going into your system and doing any kind of damage to your development. Funny ending to the story though...there wasn't any alcohol in the food. Your mother was even concerned about the type of cream or lotion she used on her skin for the fear that it contained harmful ingredients as well.

Your mother did a lot of research and reading on the internet while you were growing inside of her. It seemed as if almost every couple of days, she was calling your grandmother or me concerned about a symptom she might have for some dreaded disease. When I look back on it, I see it now as your mother was so worried to make sure you had the best start in life that she could give you. I think we went through several different types of cribs before your mother finally selected one. The reason was that they kept having recalls on the cribs for injuries to babies, and your mother wanted nothing of that. Same thing with the stroller that you'll soon be riding in. There was a recall on the one she had selected because they were pinching the fingers of babies. Your mother has been worried about you even before you were born. Get use to it. It's a family trait.

§ Chapter 5

My Turn To Be Nervous

Elizabeth called to inform us that their new car was now on its way to Harrisburg. They had found just the one they wanted, and the dealership was having it driven over to the closest location.

"You know Dad, it's coming from a place about fifteen minutes from where you grew up."

"Gee, your mother and I could have driven it there for you. An excuse to come see you."

"Yeah, that would have been good. I'm on my way to the barn and I just thought I'd call and update you."

Dad radar went up immediately.

"What do you mean you're on your way to the barn?"

The barn is actually a small horse farm where Elizabeth rides and takes lessons. She's been doing that for fifteen years.

"I'm going out to see Sylvia. I haven't seen her in a while, and Jim is working late, so I thought it would be a good time to do it."

"You certainly don't need to be around horses right now," I warned. "You don't need kicked or stepped on."

"Dad, I'm not going in the horse stalls. I'll be fine."

I've heard the "I'll be fine" routine before. Elizabeth had been taking riding lessons since she was twelve. It's a genetic memory thing again. Linda had taken riding lessons for years and must have passed it on to Elizabeth. There was a horse stable within a ten minute walk from our house in Harrisburg and Elizabeth spent a lot of her summer time there. When she went off to college her freshmen year, she tried out for the collegiate equestrian team and was selected. She was thrilled.

Her first collegiate meet was on a sunny, but brisk fall afternoon. Linda and I had traveled to just inside the New Jersey state line which ended up being about two and a half hours. Neither Linda nor I had ever been to a riding meet before, so we didn't know what to expect.

We parked in somewhat of a pasture field and walked over to an outside, fenced-in corral area where we assumed the meet would take place. There were hundreds of people milling around, and I could see signs depicting the various colleges and universities that were competing that day.

Elizabeth somehow found us, and she was already dressed in her competition garb. Let me tell you one thing about horse back riding. Most people think that once you have a horse, the big dollar items are done. I'm here to tell you that is an untruth.

Although we never purchased a horse for Elizabeth, much to her constant dismay, she still needed boots, and leggings, and a ruffled shirt, a blazer, and a black helmet, all of which are not free, and had to be replaced from time to time. And, since Elizabeth was competing in the English style riding, she had to have her own English saddle. Get the picture?

So there we were, all three of us leaning against the fence peering into the sand–covered arena to watch the first competitor. In this case, the competition was the fence jumping portion of the meet. Certainly not like the jumping competition seen on tv, the fences for this competition were more like a foot or two tall for the lesser experienced riders.

The first rider, astride her chestnut-colored horse, trotted out from the entrance gate into the center of the arena and stopped. Her name was announced over the loud speaker and she was told her time would begin now. The rider swung her horse around and trotted to the first jump. Both horse and rider cleared the fence with plenty of room to spare, and she set the horse for next jump. Another beautiful jump and the crowd applauded. It was at this point Elizabeth told us that she needed to leave and get her horse ready for the competition. We gave her a kiss, wished her luck, and she scampered off.

The rider then came down the arena near where we were standing to line up for the next jump. I could see the concentration on her face as she peered from underneath the tall black helmet.

Just as it looked like the horse was getting ready to leap, it dug its feet into the sand and stopped. The rider, however, did not. She went flying over the head of the horse and landed on her back at the base of the fence. She didn't move. The crowd became eerily quiet.

Then, a God-awful, piercing scream came from the rider as she lay stricken on the sand. Several people ran to the woman, and tried to administer first-aid. The crowd continued to look on in shock as the woman screamed out her lungs. After what seemed like an eternity, the familiar *whoop whoop* of helicopter blades filled the air. A Life Line air unit had been dispatched to the competition site and landed in another close-by field. A team of people quickly loaded the injured woman into it, and off it went.

At this point, my heart was in my throat. This was our first horse competition and we had just witnessed a major injury situation. My next thought was *no way is my little girl going in there*. I told Linda that I was going to find Elizabeth. She grabbed my arm and said she was going with me.

We wound our way through the crowd over to where we thought the competitors were prepping to go into the arena. We found Elizabeth sitting in her English saddle on her horse getting primped by her teammates. She looked so tiny while sitting in the saddle on what looked like a HUGE horse. I put my hand on the foot of her boot and looked up at her.

"Elizabeth," I started. "Are you sure you're ready to do this?"

"Yeah, Dad. Why?"

"What do you mean why? Didn't you see what just happened?" I asked.

"Yeah, but I don't do any jumping. I'm just doing the walk and trot competition."

Ok, my level of anxiety moved down a couple of notches.

"You know how to hold on tight, right?"

"Yes, Dad. I'll be fine."

So, with some trepidation, Linda and I left Elizabeth to her prepping and moved back to the spot where we had been standing along the metal fence of the corral.

Some time later, Elizabeth and her war-horse-looking mount trotted out to the center of the arena with several other competitors. In this portion of the meet, all the riders compete at the same time instead of individually like in the jumps.

The competitors started walking their horses around the inside perimeter of the corral fence. Commands were barked out over the loudspeaker for the riders to change the various gaits of their horses. After several times around the arena, all the riders were instructed to line up in the center. The awards for the different places were handed out at that point, and Elizabeth's name rang out as taking fourth place. Her teammates, who had made their way down to where Linda and I were standing, hooted and hollered at the announcement.

"Dad, are you listening to me?"

"Ah...yeah," I mumbled as I came back to reality. "You be careful."

"Yeeeesss, Dad."

I sighed. Kids.

The following day I walked into the house from the garage and saw Linda talking on the phone. She mouthed 'Elizabeth' and continued with her conversation. A short time later, she hung up the phone and chuckled.

"You should hear what those two are doing now," she started.

"Now what?" I asked as I searched through the tv channels.

"Your daughter has come up with her list of names for the baby. She said that Jim had to come up with his list as well."

"Did she mention any of the names by chance?"

"No," she replied. "They want to keep them a secret."

"You know, I'm not so sure I like all this secrecy about this and that. Holy cow, we're her family."

"Anyway," she said looking at me, "she told Jim that his list had to be done so they could compare them. So Jim is walking around the house shouting out names to see how they sound."

I looked at Linda.

"He's what?"

"He's walking around the house with his list of names and calling them out. I guess he wants to see if someone calls out the name how it will sound."

I guess when you think about it, that's not a bad idea. I remember Linda and I laying in bed talking about names. What's funny is that the name we had finally picked for Elizabeth was not the name 'Elizabeth'. Linda and I had talked about names for several weeks, and had even bought a small book of baby names and went through it trying out various names and how they sounded. We finally picked out a name and were going to tell everyone our selections for a boy and a girl.

Linda and I did have a small disagreement initially about the boy's name. If it was a boy, I wanted to name him after a major league baseball pitcher that I had really admired when I was growing up...Nolan Ryan. My logic was that we wouldn't use the name Nolan, but actually call him Ryan.

That didn't fly very far.

Anyway, we were going to announce the two names we picked. Linda had called her mother to talk it over and that's when we found out that her cousin had just adopted a little girl and used the exact two names we had picked. Who would have thought?

We couldn't have two girls with the exact names in the family, so we went back to the drawing board and came up with Elizabeth.

Looking back on it now years later, I guess it was meant to be. Although there are times when Elizabeth complained that we used a too common name. She said that when she was in third grade, there were three girls named Elizabeth in her class. They ended up using their first name and the first letter of their last name to identify each of them. It actually worked out to be Elizabeth A, B, and C. I thought it was comical, but unfortunately my eight year-old daughter didn't agree with me.

One day the following week, I got a call on my cell phone and saw that it was Linda. She rarely calls me when I'm traveling, so I figured it must be important.

"Hey, what's up?" I said into the phone.

"Are you busy right now?" Linda asked.

"No, what's going on?"

"I just got off the phone with Elizabeth. She said that when she got home for lunch today, there was a big box at the front door. She was able to drag it in and open it part of the way. She said it was a Pack n Play from Tess" (our next door neighbor).

I wasn't exactly sure what a Pack n Play was. The first thing that came to my mind was one of those DVD players that you can take in the car on trips to occupy the kids.

"Wow, that's great, but she didn't have to do that," I said. "Isn't that a little old for the baby though?"

Silence on the other end.

"Do you know what a Pack n Play is?"

"Um, isn't one of those DVD players that my brother got for the twins so they can watch movies on car trips?"

"No, it's a playpen for the baby. Don't you remember me telling you about it when I was going through Elizabeth's wish list?"

Nope, wasn't registering.

"Anyways, it's like $150! That's way too much for her to spend on the baby. She has a grandchild on the way as well."

"Have you talked to her about it yet?"

"Yeah, I just got off the phone with her. I told her it was too much, but she said that we've been such good neighbors and take care of her, and it was something she wanted to do for us."

"Well, that's very nice of her."

"Yes it is. Now we have to get something nice for her grandbaby."

I know my wife. 'Something nice' equates to a lot of money.

* * *

It's mid-January and I spent the week traveling again. My associates at work told me to dress warmly because the forecast was for very cold temperatures in the Midwest. I was in Kansas City for the week and they were exactly right. It seems the arctic jet stream dropped way down and it brought with it arctic temperatures and snow. We had snow almost every day, and temperatures reached minus five with a wind chill of minus thirty. Like I told Linda, I was never so happy to get back to the East Coast and twenty degree temperatures.

Linda picked me up on Friday evening from the airport, and instead of going straight home, we stopped at the local mall to do a little shopping. My brother's twin girls' birthday is next week, so we were looking for gifts for them. And I probably don't have to remind anyone that shopping is one of my wife's prime directives in life.

We were in one of the big name department stores and she told me about a conversation that she had with Elizabeth this past week. Elizabeth was complaining that she's getting to the point where she can't bend over and tie her shoes because of her expanding belly. She either has to sit down and tie them, or wear shoes that don't have shoestrings.

The other portion of the conversation had to do with the subject that I wanted to stay somewhat uninformed on...breast feeding and all that goes along with it. Even though I threatened to stick my fingers in my ears and sing loudly right in the middle of the girls' clothing section, Linda pressed on to tell me about the latest episode of Elizabeth's hunt for a bra that fit comfortably.

"Hey, did I tell you about Elizabeth and her new bra?" Linda started.

I was leaning against a rack of girls' clothes and pretended not to hear.

"I know you heard me," Linda continued.

"And how do you know that?" I inquired.

"Because you didn't say 'what'd you say?' she shot back.

"Ha, ha. You're so funny. No, I didn't hear about Elizabeth's new bra, but I'm sure you're going to tell me in great detail, huh?"

"Don't you want to hear about the trial and tribulations of your only daughter?"

"Yeah, but not about everything," I moaned.

"This is only about a bra. Geez, be a man."

"I'll stick my fingers in my ears and sing real loud. I mean it, right here in the girls' dresses section."

"Go ahead. I'm sure the clerks and shoppers will be very impressed at your singing ability."

A slight pause. Ok, she called my bluff.

"What about Elizabeth's new bra?" I asked sullenly.

"She's been complaining that her bras are too tight now. I told her to go find a new one that's bigger and see how it works. Well she did, and she said that the first time she put it on, it felt wonderful. She said she didn't know why it took her so long to get a different one."

"Kids," I muttered.

I thought we were done with the bra conversation. Nope, not yet.

"Elizabeth said that a woman usually increases by a couple of cup sizes when she's pregnant," Linda recited as she looked though a pile of shirts. "After she has the baby, her size goes down. If she breast feeds, then the size goes down a little, but then goes back up when her milk comes in and the baby starts feeding. I didn't know this was going on since I didn't breast feed with either of our kids. I guess the first couple of days it's actually a clear liquid called colostrum that helps with the baby's immune system."

I looked at her in amazement. This was way more information than I wanted to know.

She glanced in my direction. A smile came across her face.

"What's the matter? Too much information from your daughter?"

Ah, yeeessssss.

Linda walked in my direction, and stopped to look through a rack of girls' dresses.

"I also stopped at the baby store and looked at the crib she wants. It's going to be a little more than we anticipated."

"Gee, forgive me if I don't act surprised."

"Oh, come on Mr. Grumpy. No need to be crabby."

"So...how much is a little more?"

"Well, the crib itself is around $300. All the other stuff like bumper pads is another $140. She also wants one of those baby monitors which is another $150. So we're looking at about $600 total."

"Wow, why is the baby monitor so much? Isn't it just one of those walkie-talkie things so you can hear the baby if it cries?"

"Oh you're so 1980's. It has a pad that goes under the baby that monitors its movements and breathing," she replied.

I just shook my head.

"Well, it looks like I'm going to have to go down to the blood bank and give more plasma, huh?" I replied.

"No, nothing that drastic yet. I've been putting away a little bit here and there, and we have just about the right amount now."

My wife is always so good at those things.

"Good, I'm not so sure I could take those needles again," I said. "Ready for some Chinese food?"

"You bet," came her quick reply.

* * *

Did you ever get out of bed in the morning and something was telling you that you're about to have a bad day? Well, that happened to me one day on my last business trip. I'm not a big

80

believer that if something happens or doesn't happen, it's an omen of things to come; but I have to tell you, now that I look back on that morning, I could certainly make an argument for it.

I was a little on edge anyway. Linda was scheduled for a stress test for potential heart problems because of some pain she was having in her chest, so I didn't get a very good night's sleep being 900 miles away. My shoelace broke when I was tying my shoe, I didn't have enough milk for cereal (I know, boo hoo), and I forgot my piece of fruit for my mid-morning snack.

I got into work and did my routine checks, and everything was running normal up until my 8 am meeting with my senior leadership team. One of my senior leaders asked to stay afterwards because she had some personnel items to discuss. After a few minutes of talking about a couple of her associates, she pulled out a sealed envelope with my name written on it and laid it on my desk. I looked at her and said that the envelope had better contain a wedding invitation. Unfortunately, it did not. It was her two week resignation letter. We discussed her reasoning, the exit strategy and communication plan for her departure, and then I had to discuss it with the vice president of our human resources department.

I no sooner get done with that discussion and my cell phone rang. I looked at the number and it's Linda. I know it had nothing to do with her stress test because it was an hour away yet.

"Hey, what's going on?" I asked hesitantly.

"Are you in the middle of something?"

"No, no, go ahead."

"I'm on my way to do my stress test and I wanted to tell you about a conversation I just had with Elizabeth," Linda said.

Now what.

"She's going to the doctor's because she's been having strong contractions on a regular basis, and the doctor wants to see her. I'm sure it's Braxton-Hicks syndrome, but the doctor wants to see her."

Braxton-Hicks....hmmm. I'm not even sure I can spell that let alone know what it is.

"I just wanted to let you know in case she calls when she's done. I'll still be in the stress test and I didn't want this hitting you without telling you."

"Well, good, I'm glad you did tell me. Geez, the two most

important women in my life and you both have medical issues, and I'm 900 miles away."

"We'll be fine."

"I know, just call me when you're done. I'll have my phone with me all day, even when I work out during lunch, so call me."

"I will, love you."

"I love you too."

And the phone went silent.

I turned to my computer and went straight to the internet. I pulled up the handiest website I know for these types of problems...WebMD, and typed in Braxton. Luckily I spelled it right and the site went right to the definition and symptoms.

Braxton-Hicks is also known as "false labor" pains, and is the way a woman's body gets ready for the real thing. As I read down through the article, most of it was reassuring that it truly is nothing to be greatly concerned about. There were one or two items that had a slight cause for concern, like see your doctor if the contractions are regular and you're less than thirty-two weeks. Bingo.

Just as I was finishing reading the article, it was time to head to lunch, or in my case, the gym. I had a lot of nervous energy to run off even though I was tired. I happened to mention my conversation with Linda to my administrative assistant as I walked into the outer office, and she remarked that she had the same problem, and she knows a lot of women who also had this. She was reassuring that there are medications that will work on the contractions. So I drove to the gym with my stress level a few notches lower.

I had changed and was running on the treadmill and my cell phone rang.

"Hi Elizabeth," I said a little out of breath.

"Hi Dad," she replied quietly.

"So tell me all about it," I said trying to calm my breathing down.

"I'm on bed rest until Monday. They want me to take it easy for few days and see if that helps. I'm lying on the couch right now."

"Well that's good," I said trying to sound cheerful.

"They also put me on a medication that will stop the false contractions. I don't remember the exact name, but they also prescribe it for asthma."

"Really?"

"Yeah, they said it could make me jittery. Now tell me, how is a drug that could make me jittery supposed to calm me down and the stop the contractions?"

"I'm not exactly sure," I replied still trying to sound cheerful.

"Dad, I was hoping that I would fly through this pregnancy and not have any problems. Now look at me."

"Oh honey, it's ok. You may have been overdoing it. I think it was smart for you to recognize the problem and then call the doctor to see what to do."

"Yeah, I know. I'll tell you this though. I am not having this baby until it's time. I've already got my mind made up."

"Well, that's good, but you're only half of the equation. The little one is the other half."

"That's true. I go back to the doctor on Friday and they do some type of test to check the amniotic fluid to make sure there's enough. I guess that's also one of the things that can trigger this."

"Honey, for the time being, just relax. Take it easy. Live the good life. Pretty soon you're going to begging for some down time."

"I'm trying, but there's nothing on television."

"Tell you what, I was running when you called, so how about I call you later tonight?"

"Yep, that's good."

"Ok, talk with you later. Remember, relax."

"Ok dad."

I folded the phone and began running again. I was five minutes into it, and my cell phone rang again. It was Linda.

"Hello," I said very out of breath.

"It's just me. I know you're working out, and that you spoke with Elizabeth, because I just talked with her, so I'll keep it short."

"No, tell me how your test went."

"I guess it went ok. I'm assuming that if there was anything really bad, they would have said something."

"Yeah, but the techs aren't really allowed to tell you anything," I countered.

"The doctor was there the whole time. She watched me through the entire test."

Ok, now I feel a little better.

"Did they make you do the treadmill where it goes higher and faster?" I inquire.

"Yeah. They kept telling me to take longer strides, and I told them that I'm just a little person with little legs."

My wife doesn't technically fit the strict definition of a little person. She's actually just a smidge under five feet, as is Elizabeth.

"How many minutes did you go?"

"I don't know. I didn't ask."

"So what are you going to do now?"

"I need some CAFFEINE! I haven't had any since yesterday morning."

"Well, go get some caffeine and I'll call you later tonight. I'm glad everything went well for you."

"Me too."

"Hey, Elizabeth said that there's no way she's having this baby before it's due," I said.

"She is so stubborn," came the reply from the phone.

"And who does that sound like?" I questioned.

"Not me, I wasn't like that when I was pregnant."

"Oh, I agree with that. It's just all the other times," I said with a laugh.

"Am not."

"See? And you say you're not stubborn."

"It's the lack of caffeine. I'll talk with you later tonight."

And the phone went silent once again.

I got back onto the treadmill with a renewed sense of well-being. We had weathered more situations and they ended well, at least until now. I'll have to wait and see what other adventures life throws at us as we navigate the final eight weeks of the pregnancy.

Later on in the evening, as I do every evening, I called Linda and talked about how her afternoon and evening went.

"I ended up going to Babies R Us to order the crib. I wanted to look at it and see if it was what Elizabeth wanted."

"How are we going to get it to them?"

Well, my first thought was to ship it from the store to their house, but they charge for shipping. The girl who checked me out, she was very nice, told me that they could ship it to a Toys R Us or Babies R Us free of charge, and they could pick it up there."

"Cool, is that what you did?"

"Yes, but not until I checked with Elizabeth first. As jumpy as she is right now, I didn't want to agree to something and her not like it. Since they go to the hospital on Wednesdays now, and the Toys R US is right near there, it shouldn't be a problem. And she agreed. Imagine that?"

"Good. What else did you buy?"

"You know, that store is so overwhelming. I had printed out Elizabeth's list from Amazon and walked around picking up the small stuff on the list, and then I stopped. I remembered that I had an old list, so I printed out a new one at the store, and you know what? Everything I had picked was already gone from the list, so I put it all back."

Disaster avoided.

"So I left the store and called Elizabeth. You know, I called her probably three or four times today. She said that she was getting calls all day from people."

"She's just lying on the couch. No stress."

"She told me that she looked up the medication she's taking on-line. She said that she's not taking it anymore until she talks with the doctor. Evidently she read that it has some side effects."

"Oh geez. How did she get on-line? The computer is upstairs."

"Jim brought home a laptop from work so she could use the computer. She said that the side effects were from women who had taken it for a long period of time, but she said she's not taking any chances. She also said that she feels much better now that's she's taking it easier."

"I guess that's good."

"Well, it's getting pretty late, and I have some things to do yet. I'll talk with you tomorrow."

"Ok, I guess we'll wait on the report from Elizabeth tomorrow on how her conversation went with the doctor, huh?"

"Oh yeah. Can't wait for that one."

I got a report from Linda that next night that Elizabeth's test for the amniotic fluid went fine. The baby was developing right along schedule, and was getting into position for the birth canal. The contractions were still occurring, but not as intense or as frequent as before. Elizabeth was still very stubborn about not taking the medication for the contractions. She felt that as long as she is resting, the contractions subside for the most part. She has another appointment tomorrow with the doctor. Linda and I are both wondering how the doctor will react when he hears that she is not taking the medication. My daughter might be small in stature, but she is very tough. Always has been.

She played a year of field hockey in high school and seemed to be always in the penalty box for being too aggressive or using her hockey stick in an unladylike-like way. She had to end her field hockey career after one year because playing in the high school marching band was the same time as for field hockey, and she couldn't do both. I'm thinking the opposing players were thankful.

Linda also told me about her gift that she had selected for Elizabeth's baby shower which is in a week.

"I was looking at the calendar today and saw that the shower was in a week. I freaked because I still hadn't gotten her a gift. So I went on line and looked up those rubber balloon bumpers for the crib. I know they were a lot of money, but I went ahead and bought them. Remember we looked at them at the baby store?"

"Those were the $200 bumpers, right?" I asked.

"Yeah, I know they were expensive, but that's what she wanted," Linda replied.

"She also wanted a horse, but we didn't get that for her," I responded.

"This is different, this is our grandchild," she said.

"Ok, so let's add up the total score for this crib. How much was the final tally for the crib?" I said aloud.

"$300. But the shipping was free."

"And how much was the mattress?"

"$125. That was on sale though."

And what was the cost for the rubber baby buggy bouncers?"

"Say $215 for round figures."

"So, the grand total for this crib is $640. My, oh my. Does it heat the bottle and then burp the baby?"

"You would think so for that price."

"Boy, I hope our daughter realizes how much we love her."

"I'm sure she does."

"Well, at least $640 worth."

* * *

I finally made the decision to look for another job in the Pittsburgh area. I have been traveling back and forth between Pittsburgh and Kansas City for over three years, and I'm tired. I spoke to my boss about it and he was very understanding and supportive. It didn't really dawn on him until we discussed it that I had been doing this for over three years. Since the lease on the apartment in Kansas City is up in May, that will give both the company and me about three and a half months to make the transition.

The thing is, when I agreed to come back to work at the company and travel back and forth, I said I would do it for a couple of months, maybe up to six months at the outside. Well, six months turned into three years. I really like the company, and the people I work with, so it was no big deal, but it's now time for me to do something locally. With the baby due next month, I want more time at home so Linda and I can make the trip to Harrisburg whenever we want. Right now, we can't do that because I'm either coming back from a trip, or getting ready to leave. It really constricts us on what and when we can do things.

It's both an exciting and anxious time for me. I look forward to moving on to another company and meeting new people, but at the same time, I am nervous about the whole situation. Linda and I had a discussion this morning about the 'what ifs', and we worked out a plan. I'll continue to work with the headhunters and sending out resumes until I find something that I like. My wife wonders if I should have waited until the baby arrived. Nothing like living on the edge.

Ryan received some bad news from one of his friends who still lives back in Harrisburg. His friend's mother had died this past week, and he wanted Ryan to come out to the funeral which is this Saturday. The tough thing about it was that there was over thirty inches of snow on the ground, and traveling in the mountains of Pennsylvania can be treacherous. I know from prior experience.

I talked with Ryan throughout the week about road conditions and the possibility of not going to the funeral. He sounded like he was agreeing to it all. That's a first. I just spoke with him yesterday and he said that he had packed a bag and was going to watch the weather and make his decision in the morning.

Last night, I was sitting at the computer finishing up some

work and the house phone rang. I recognized the number on the display as Ryan's

"Hey Dad, what's up?"

"Nothing, just sitting here at the computer and doing some work. What are you doing?"

A slight pause.

"I'm on the turnpike about thirty minutes from Harrisburg."

My turn for a slight pause.

"You're what?" I asked.

"I'm just about to Joey's house."

"I didn't think you were going to leave until tomorrow?"

"Well," he said, "I didn't have to work today, and instead of sitting around all day, I thought that I would just leave."

"How were the roads?"

"They were good until I got into the mountains. It was really snowing. I could hardly see anything. We all slowed down to forty-five."

"Any problems?"

"Nope," he answered. "I even brought along some extra anti-freeze and windshield wash fluid."

"That's good. Did you call your sister and let her know that you'll be in town?"

"Yeah, just before I called you. She sounded surprised that I was coming in."

"I think your mother was supposed to tell her that, but I don't know. Make sure you at least stop in and say hello."

"Yeah, I will. I'm parking my car there. Joey doesn't think that my car will make it up his driveway with all the snow. He's coming to pick me up."

"Ok, just be careful. Nothing silly, ok? You be the designated driver."

"Don't worry Dad. Nothing silly."

Just as Linda and I were getting ready to go shopping for some cabinets for the sewing room the following morning, her phone rang.

"Hey Elizabeth, what's going on?" I said into the receiver.

"Nothing. I'm waiting or Jim to come back from doing some errands and then we're going up to the mall."

"Oh, what errands is Jim doing?"

"His parents are in Pittsburgh this weekend, and he's picking up their mail and stuff like that. Hey, did you hear about my latest appointment?"

"No, what week are in you in by the way?"

"It's week thirty-four. I had my latest ultrasound and the doctor showed me the baby. He said I should be having a lot of movement, and boy I am."

"What was the appointment all about? I asked.

"I go every week now, so I get an ultrasound done more often. The doctor showed me that the baby's head is pointing down and getting set up for birth. The butt is on my right side underneath my right ribcage. The feet are underneath my left ribcage and from time to time, you can see them pointing out in my belly."

"Cool, I remember when you were doing that with your mother," I replied.

"The doctor said I can go back to work on February twenty-eighth. I'm at thirty-six weeks at that point, and the baby can live outside the womb then because the lungs are fully formed."

"Oh really?"

"Yeah, they've said several times that I need to be at thirty-six weeks before I can go off the medicine, or go back to work, or both," she said laughing.

"Looking forward to going back to work?"

"I don't think so," she said. "I'm getting use to being at home and working just a couple of hours a day."

"So when you have the baby, how much time are you taking off before you go back?"

"Dad, I'm not going back full time. I'm going to work part-time from the house. Don't you remember me telling you that?"

A grimace crossed my face, and I kicked myself mentally.

"Yeah, now that you say that, I do remember."

"Hey different subject. Have you talked with Ryan today?"

"No. He stopped in for about an hour last night, and then Joey came and picked him up. I think the funeral is at two this afternoon."

"Oh, ok. I didn't know that. When he called last night, he wasn't at Joey's yet, so he didn't know what time everything was going to happen."

"I haven't talked with him today."

"We'll call him later, and see what he's doing. I'm a little concerned that he's driving back later in the day. We're supposed to get a little bit of snow, but you know they get more in the mountains. And with his beater of a car, I just want to make sure he knows."

"Yeah, I know."

"I'm going to go jump in the shower. Do you want to talk with you mother?"

"Do you think she has time for me?" she asked giggling.

"Ha, ha. I think she'll be able to squeeze you into her schedule."

I went up the stairs and made a noisy entrance into the bedroom.

"Your daughter is on the phone."

§ Chapter **6**

Our Pre-Natal Odysseys

Since Elizabeth and Jim live on the other side of
Pennsylvania, and with me out of town every other week, we rarely
get a weekend free to make the trip across the state; however, we
were able to get a few trips in before the baby was born

* * *

Elizabeth called from Ocean City, Maryland. She and Jim
had joined Jim's family for a few days at a rental condo on a beach
in Maryland. Jim's oldest brother and his family, and his parents,
had all chipped in for a portion of the week's rent, and were
spending a few days of relaxation before school started for the
older kids. I asked Elizabeth if they had told Jim's brother and wife
about the pregnancy.
        "Oh yeah, as soon as we walked in the door, Jim told them,"
she replied. "I didn't even get chance to get a word in."
        "What did they say when they heard?" I ask.
        "Oh you know, the usual 'that's great", and hugs."
        "How was the trip down?" I ask. (I know the way very well
since I traveled there weekly for eighteen months as an account
manager for a large customer.)
        "We left at 6:30 am. It was such a long trip. We went
through Delaware and stopped at a McDonald's for breakfast. As
soon as I walked in, I got sick. I didn't throw up or anything, just a

real queasy stomach. I ended up going back to the car and slept for most of the time until we got here."

"Are you ok now?"

"Yeah, we got here and went right to the beach. The fresh salt air seemed to do the trick."

"Good, glad you made it there safely. You're mother is standing right here, so I'll give the phone over to her. Just be careful."

I handed the phone over to my wife who began the conversation with the same basic questions I did. I smiled and shook my head. Seemed like she had the same conversation with each of us, but I'm sure Elizabeth doesn't mind. She's been doing it for the last five years.

While my daughter and son-in-law are basking in the sun on the white sandy beaches of Atlantic City, I will be working to set up a resupply mission. Well, it's not really a resupply mission, but it certainly feels like one.

Since my in-laws' house is on the market, we've made several trips there to clean out all the things that were accumulated over fifty-two years of living there, taking care of the yard work, and doing some general repairs to make it look presentable for any perspective buyers. There were just a few things left in the house and my wife and I took some vacation time to make a final run to get those things out. I have rented a truck for several days, will travel the two hours from our house to the in-laws, and then load up a sofa, easy chair, freezer, and hutch. We then make the four hour trek to my daughter's house, unload the freezer and hutch, and then drive to our son's apartment and unload the sofa and easy chair.

And if I have any strength and energy left, I'll return the truck and collapse.

We made it to our daughter's house around supper time. Both of them were very hungry, so my wife and Elizabeth went to get a pizza and Jim and I unloaded the furniture from the rental truck. We were able to get all the furniture off the truck in a relatively short time. We had put all of it in the right place by the time the girls arrived back with the pizza.

As we were sitting around the table eating and talking, Elizabeth told us a story from when they were at the beach just a few days ago.

"I've had such bad constipation since I've been pregnant," she began. "It really hit me the one day we went for a stroll on the boardwalk."

"We were staying at a condo on 37th street, so we ended up driving down to the boardwalk and, since there were six adults and two kids, we decided to take two cars. We all made it there together and decided to split up for a while and go our separate ways because people wanted to do different things."

"Jim and I were walking along and I got this sharp gas pain. I tried not to let on, so we kept walking. The pain was starting to get worse, so I looked at Jim and told him I needed to go back to the condo...now"

"Jim looked at me and asked why. I said that I needed to go back and use the bathroom, because, well...you know. Jim said something like 'Ah, ok, I understand', and he called his mother on his cell phone to see if we could use their car since we didn't drive. I heard Jim talking and say "Elizabeth doesn't feel good, so we need to go back"'.

Jim broke in, "It was at this point, everyone decided to go back together. As we're walking to the car, my mother kept asking me what was wrong with Elizabeth, and I finally said that you'll have to ask her."

"Yeah," Elizabeth said. "She said stuff like, 'is it your stomach, or do you have heartburn', so I finally told her that I was really constipated. She said 'oh you poor dear,' and we dropped it. Just as we're getting into the car, Jim's dad puts his arm around me and whispered in my ear, 'Don't worry, Susan was like that with all three of our kids.'"

I asked, "So did everyone go back to the condo with you?"

Elizabeth laughed. "Yes, everyone was there waiting for me. I felt like I was performing."

"You didn't have performance anxiety, did you?" I asked laughing.

"Very funny Dad, but I did manage to gain a partial victory, at least that's what I told everyone, and they all cheered when I came out, even the kids."

At this point, everyone had tears in their eyes from laughing so hard. My wife gets into one of these hysteria moods when she hears a funny story and the act of laughing and seeing other people laugh makes her laugh even more. This usually occurs when she's very tired, and such was the case that night. So there is my wife laughing hysterically which is causing the rest of us to laugh which causes her to laugh even more. It's one of those vicious circle kinds of things.

Finally, my stomach hurt so much from laughing, and I couldn't take it anymore. We all finally calmed down, but this is one of those tense sessions like cowboys dealing with the threat of a cattle stampede; any little thing could set if off. Just as we had regained our composure, Elizabeth's cat made an entrance into the living room.

Now this cat has the demeanor of a gremlin from hell, hence her nickname of the cat from hell. She is a feral cat and the only person that can get close to her is Elizabeth. Anyone else who gets close enough to try and pet her is met with a hiss and a swat from a paw. Elizabeth got her as a small kitten and raised her in an apartment where she was not supposed to have any animals. The cat had the run of the place night and day and pretty much did whatever she desired. My daughter has a big, soft heart when it comes to animals and Chloe the cat took full advantage of that.

It was also a general belief held by our family that Chloe had been dropped on her head when she was young. For example, her favorite bed was the bathroom sink. Elizabeth would find her curled up asleep in the bathroom sink each morning. Once Elizabeth shooed her out, Chloe would find her way in with Elizabeth to hang out in the shower. No one had ever seen a cat that enjoyed water as much as her. Little did I know that was just one of the odd things that I would learn about her.

My wife and I stayed at Elizabeth's apartment one night when I was in town for business. Elizabeth was in a wedding several hours away, and had to stay overnight, so we had her apartment to ourselves. Unbeknownst to us, that's when the cat's real fun begins.

Being used to a queen-sized bed, my wife and I squeezed into Elizabeth's regular double bed and, trying to abide by our daughter's wishes, turned off the window unit air conditioner in the living room. It was August, and the apartment was on the second floor. It wasn't too long before it got stuffy.

After tossing back and forth (and sweating) for what seemed an eternity, I finally found sleep. It was very relaxing and felt great. It was then that I had a sense of foreboding. Did you ever get that feeling that you were being watched by someone or something, and it made you feel creepy? Welcome to my next few hours.

I opened my eyes, and there not an inch from my face, stared Chloe with those big, yellow eyes. She was perched on the night stand next to the bed, leaning over and just staring at me in the darkness. I pushed her away and she jumped down off the nightstand and ran out the bedroom door into the living room. I think I heard her giggling as she left.

Over the course of the next few hours, Chloe and I did a silent battle of wills. She would jump onto the bed, and walk around. I would shoo her off, only to fall back to sleep for a short time and we'd start all over again. After reflecting on this situation about a year later, I'd have to give that round to Chloe. Everything that my wife and I tried to calm her down, or keep her out of the bedroom, failed miserably. We ended up getting about five hours of interrupted sleep that night. One side note: I had to go to work the next morning, while my wife and Chloe got to sleep in and nap during the day.

Oh, the joy of family.

Well Chloe marches into the living room and plops down in the center of the floor. Hanging out of her mouth is one of my daughter's stretchy hair ties. She steals them from my daughter's dresser. You can spot them all through the house.

"Watch this Dad. You're going to flip," remarks Elizabeth.

Chloe is still holding the hair tie in her mouth and wriggled one of her hind legs up and stretched out the hair tie. She let go of the end in her mouth and the hair tie went flying across the room. She jumped up and chased after it, and repeated the whole process again.

That was the spark that started the stampede. My wife found this so funny that the laughing hysteria snuck back into the room. We all laughed until there were tears on everyone's face. My wife actually left the room to try and stop laughing. This was one of those special times when you realize just how much your family means to you.

I also learned some things on this trip to my daughter's house. She and my wife went shopping during the full day of our visit and came home carrying several stuffed shopping bags.

"Hey Dad, want to see what we bought?" inquired Elizabeth

as she placed the bags on the floor next to the couch.

"Sure, I always like to see where my money goes," I replied.

"How do you know Mom bought anything?"

I turn to my wife and was met with a feigned look of innocence.

"Your mother didn't drive five hours to go shopping with you and not spend any money. Right?" as I looked at my wife.

"I'm staying out of this," she said. "It's between you two."

Elizabeth reached into the first bag and pulled out what looked to be a folded pair of jeans. They looked ok to me. And then Elizabeth held them up and showed the front of the pants.

"Ah, you got your first pair of maternity jeans, huh?" I asked.

"Maternity clothes have really changed since I was pregnant with Elizabeth," said my wife.

"Yeah, they now have under belly, mid belly, and above belly maternity clothes," said Elizabeth.

"Geez, why did you need all of those different kinds?"

"Women carry their babies differently. Some women carry babies low, some carry just out in front, and some carry their babies high on their belly. That's why we need the different types of jeans," explained Elizabeth.

Silly me.

We went through the first bag of clothes which turned out to be maternity shirts and more maternity pants. No wait, sorry. They are maternity *tops and slacks*.

"What's in the other bag?" I asked innocently.

"Oh, just some maternity bras. Want to see them?" asked my daughter, grinning.

I stopped and thought just for a moment before answering the question. I had always thought of myself as a pretty open parent with my children as they were growing up. I always taught them that they could come to me with any problem on any subject and never be embarrassed talking about it with me.

"No, I think I'll pass."

That may have worked when they were five, but not when they're twenty-seven and pregnant. Come to think of it, it didn't worked very well when they five either.

Probably time to see what's on ESPN.

Later that night, my wife and I took Elizabeth and Jim out to dinner. We made it into the restaurant without Elizabeth going into any seizures at the smell of cooked food. While we were sitting in the booth making small talk before our food arrived, I asked Elizabeth if we could now tell family members of the baby coming.

"No, not yet," she replied.

"Why not? It's after the twelfth week," I countered.

"I have a doctor's appointment next Wednesday, and if everything is ok, then you can tell people."

"Are you having another one of those ultra-sounds again?"

"No, it's another Doppler test."

"Geez Elizabeth, this baby is going to come out vibrating with the amount of sound waves passing through its body."

*　*　*

If you remember back a couple of months ago, my wife and I rented a truck to take out some furniture to Elizabeth to help furnish the nursery. I had a completely loaded truck with dressers, mirrors, chairs, and other assorted smaller furniture items that could fit in the nooks and crannies. Jim and I had unloaded all the furniture and placed it very neatly in their garage, trying to make room for both their cars.

After looking over the freshly unloaded furniture, Elizabeth announced that she did not want one dresser because "it didn't match the other furniture in the nursery."

Jim and I were standing at the open end of the garage, soaked with sweat due to the hot August afternoon, watching Elizabeth and Linda. Linda threw a glance our way that basically said 'don't get upset, let me talk with her.'

"Now Elizabeth, remember, you're going to need the room because a baby has a lot of clothes. This dresser is ok even if it's darker than other furniture. You can put it in a closet for more storage space. I did that with your baby stuff."

"Mom, I really want all the furniture to match," Elizabeth protested. "I have no where to store it since we don't have a basement. Couldn't you and Dad take it back home to store it, and maybe bring it back in January or February?"

"This time is going to go by faster than you think," Linda countered. "I can't guarantee when your Father and I can get this back to you."

"That's ok. I really don't think I need it."

And with that, Jim and I moved several pieces of furniture to get to the dresser, dragged it out, and loaded it back on the truck. I got the dresser back to our house, wrestled it off the truck, and put it in our garage.

Not twenty-four hours later, Elizabeth called and said she had reconsidered, and now wanted the dresser back. I tell you all this because this is the week that we are making the trek back to Harrisburg with the dresser. I took vacation this week to get some things done around the house (plus I was going to lose the vacation if I didn't take it), go to my in-law's house to get it ready for winter, and then take the dresser to Elizabeth.

This was a well traveled dresser. It started at my in-law's house in north central Pennsylvania, rode to Harrisburg where it was deemed unfit by my daughter, then transported to Pittsburgh where it sat in my garage for two months. It's now going from Pittsburgh back to north central Pennsylvania (and sit in my SUV until the in-law's house is winterized), and then taken to Harrisburg where it will hopefully reside for many years.

It's a good thing I love my daughter.

While we were at my in-law's house, we had the occasion to eat dinner with some close relatives. They are cousins on my wife's side and are just a few years older than us. They have a daughter that they adopted about six months before Elizabeth was born, and also have a granddaughter that was born about five months ago. There's a lot we have in common, and we enjoy a good time whenever we get together. Plus they have just retired after many years as teachers and administrators in the local school system, and this is their first autumn of not having to go back to school.

During dinner, cell phones from both sides of the family were ringing regularly with updates from various children. Once such call was from Elizabeth around 8:30 pm. I happened to answer the call.

"Hi Elizabeth, how are you?" I started.

"Hey Day, I'm good. What are you and Mom doing?"

"We're having dinner with Jack and Gloria," I replied. "What are you doing?"

"Oh sorry, I didn't know. I just got back from a class."

"Class? What kind of class?"

"It was my first class on breast feeding. Geez Dad, there's a whole lot more to it that I thought. I have to −"

I interrupted. "Wait Elizabeth, um, this is probably something you want to tell your Mother about, right?"

"Well, yeah, but don't you want to hear about it?"

"I'll tell you what. I'll have your Mother call you when we get back to the house. How's that?"

"Ok, that's fine," she said.

We tried calling a little later, but the phone went right to her voice mail. I'm sure she was tired and was in bed already.

And gee, I really wanted to hear about breast feeding too.

The next evening Elizabeth called on her way home from work. Linda was taking a long, hot shower since we had raked, weeded, dug, hoed, and bagged various plants and fauna all day.

I picked up the phone.

"Hey, what are you doing?" I asked.

"Oh, just driving home from work," came the statically reply. "I have to get dinner going quick. Jim and I have a registration class at the hospital tonight."

"Another class? Bet you didn't think there was so much studying in having a baby?" I asked laughing.

"This one is a required class. Everyone has to do this before you can get registered to have the baby at this hospital."

"Really? I guess not one more baby will be delivered until the paperwork is done, huh?"

"Yeah, it certainly sounds something like that. I just wanted to let you know that I did see that you called last night, but I was really tired. I'm sorry I missed your call."

"Oh, no problem. Your mother and I thought it was something like. We'll see you tomorrow."

"Ok, Dad, you and Mom travel safely."

Linda and I set out for the four hour ride to Elizabeth and Jim's house around one in the afternoon. It was a spectacular day in Pennsylvania for early November. The sun was bright and warm, temperature was in the mid-sixties, and there was not a cloud in the sky. We repacked the SUV and headed southeast towards Harrisburg.

Linda stayed awake the entire trip. Somewhat of a rarity. After she gets her belly full, with the sun streaming through the windows, and the relaxing car vibrations, it's usually off to sleepy time within the first hour of the trip. She was pretty alert and talkative the whole way.

We arrived into Harrisburg around five that evening. After several cell phone calls, and being volunteered to get something for dinner, we stopped at the supermarket, and finally got to Elizabeth and Jim's house around five thirty. By the time we arrived, it had clouded over and a light drizzle was falling. I decided that we would wait until the next morning to unload the dresser. No sense trying to mess with it in the dark.

Surprisingly, Elizabeth was not at home when we arrived. Her boss had asked her to stay over a few minutes to work on some last minute changes that had come up. She got to the house around 5:45 pm and was somewhat perturbed at having to stay over, especially on a Friday.

When she came through the door, the reality of the upcoming baby became very apparent to me. She was wearing a maternity top and her expanding belly was showing itself. It was sight to behold. My beautiful blond haired, blue eyed daughter was carrying the next generation of our family.

She bounded upstairs, as much as a five month pregnant woman can, and quickly changed into more comfortable clothing. In this case, pajamas, and joined the rest of us in the kitchen where we were preparing dinner.

Elizabeth stood next to the counter with Jim while her mother and I peeled potatoes and squash. She was a little calmer at this point having already expounded on the reasons for being late, and had then launched into a discussion about her breast feeding class. Right in the middle of her narrative, she looked at Jim.

"Did your mother breast feed you?" she inquired.

A look of horror crossed his face. He looked as if he had been shot.

"I...ah...um...she..."

I interrupted.

"I bet it never came up in the course of general conversation, did it?"

He let out a big sigh.

"No, it never did."

"And make sure you wipe out any mental picture you had," I added.

We all laughed as the color returned to Jim's face.

After dinner was in the oven, we all went to the living room to relax and watch some television. We were all pretty bushed from the week and not much was said.

Dinner was very good. I made some killer butternut squash. I used Jim's hand blender, and the squash came out more like soup, but it tasted good.

I watched my daughter while she ate. Her skin was clear and glowing, her hair was smooth and shiny. It really is true that women take on a beautiful radiance when they are pregnant. It had been so long since I had been around a pregnant woman for any length of time that I had forgotten it.

Things don't move very fast in the morning at my daughter's house, and add in my wife who also doesn't like mornings, and that can make it even slower. Elizabeth and Jim like to lounge around the house in their pajamas until noon and then decide what they will do for the day (I am somewhat joking, but not much.) It was Saturday, so I really couldn't blame them. As I have always been an early riser, this creates minor conflicts at times with members of my family.

Our plan for the day was to spend time with Elizabeth and Jim until lunch and then head for home but, as I had expected, that was not to be.

At about 10 am (half the day is gone), Elizabeth offered that we all go out for breakfast at a diner in town that none of us had ever been to before. As with mornings, breakfast is not a big item with any of them either, except with me. At this point, I was starving while waiting to see what the family wanted to do. After some discussion, we decided not to go out for breakfast, but instead, go shopping at the nearby mall and have lunch out. My daughter always seemed to work that into the plan of the day whenever we're there. With that monumental decision out of the way, I grabbed a box of the nearest cereal and scarfed down two huge bowls. I felt much better and could now face the day.

While they were having their second and third cups of their favorite morning beverage, I needed to get up and do something. My taste in television programming is not anywhere near my daughter's or son-in-law's taste, and I was tired of watching food show reruns waiting for them to get up enough energy to get dressed.

I went out into the garage and made space for the dresser. We had not unloaded it from the SUV because of the rain the previous night. It wasn't raining now, but it was gloomy and cold, and it looked like the skies could open up at any minute. I had originally thought of asking Jim for some help, but instead, decided that I could do it myself.

I was able to wrestle the dresser out of the vehicle and get it in place to where there was space in the garage. I tried to put it in an out of the way place so that neither of their cars would hit it.

I went back into the house and found that the kids had finally generated enough body energy to go upstairs and get dressed. Linda also gets a little antsy after some time of inactivity, and she was actually showered and dressed, sitting in the living room playing with the cat. Just a side note, you never really play with Chloe the devil cat. It's more like she allows time for you to gaze upon her.

After another hour, Elizabeth and Jim finally declared they were ready to venture outside into the world. We all squeezed into Jim's 1993 compact car and headed for the mall.

Usually excursions to the mall end up costing me money, and this time was no different. The girls did some light shopping (only two bags of maternity clothes) while Jim and I sat on the benches outside each of the stores and talked guy stuff.

After the long discussion in the morning of eating arrangements, we ended up eating in the food court at the mall. Don't get me wrong, food court food is okay, but Elizabeth's taste is usually more of the sit down and dine restaurant variety. I certainly didn't complain at that point. I ended up getting Chinese while every one else opted for Italian.

I love to people watch, especially in the mall. You can see people from all walks of life scurrying up and down the wide expanses. The food court is no different and is often more entertaining because folks are relatively still instead of just passer-bys.

I spied a family that had just sat down several tables from us with a baby that was probably eighteen months old. She was sitting on the table being steadied by her mother. There looked to be a father, two older siblings, and a grandmother. Everyone else got up from the table except the baby and grandmother. The baby had been placed on the table in front of the grandmother who was now holding onto the legs. She was cooing to the baby and getting some pretty comical responses in the forms of facial expressions and laughter. There were oblivious to everyone else in the food court, and their whole world was focused on just each other. I moved the grandmother out of the picture and placed my wife into it, and tried to visualize what that scene would look like in a couple of years.

I could see Linda sitting there with our grandchild, both of them looking beautiful together. Much like the scene here, they were focused solely on each other, and no one else was in their world. Linda was laughing at the antics of the baby, and you could see and feel the love between them.

I was snapped back into reality with a tap on the shoulder from Linda.

"Where were you?" she asked.

"What do you mean?" I countered.

"I was asking if you were ready to go, and you seemed like you were in a different world."

"For a while I was. I was just watching the table over there with the baby and grandmother," I said.

"Yeah, I saw them too. They're cute together," Linda said softly as she shifted her eyes to the other table.

"Ok, let's go. We're way behind schedule now."

After our good byes to Elizabeth and Jim (and minus one dresser), Linda and I made it back to Pittsburgh in a relative good time. Linda wasn't as staunch this time in the car. There was plenty of good sleepy time.

*   *   *

It's getting closer to the due date, and Elizabeth's friends in Harrisburg put together a baby shower. Linda left yesterday for Elizabeth's house to be there in time for the baby shower. It was a bright and sunny, but very cold, day and the roads were clear.

I called her later in the evening to see how things were going. I called her cell phone and it rang and rang, and finally went to the voice mail. Not unusual for Linda. She puts down her phone all over the house and then wanders around looking for it. I called Elizabeth's phone and after two rings, she picked up.

"You know, you got me yelled at because I had to get off the couch to answer the phone," Elizabeth said.

"If your mother would keep the phone with her, we wouldn't

103

run into these problems."

"Yeah, I know. She's upstairs making the bed."

"So tell me how things are going. How's Jim?"

"Oh, he's fine. He's actually out picking up my prescription."

"You've decided to take the contraction medication? What changed your mind?"

"The doctor was pretty firm in that I should take the medication. He said that if I didn't, the chances of me having a pre-mature baby increased, and that was not good. He said that the risks of having a pre-mature baby with lots of problems far outweighed the risk of the side effects."

"You know, that's what you're mother and I discussed a couple of nights ago."

"Probably the main thing that changed my mind," she continued, "was the nurse at the hospital, you know, the one where we're taking baby classes."

"Oh really? Why?"

"We missed last week's class because that was the day that I was put on bed rest, and I had forgotten to ask the doctor if I could go. I called and left her a message about why we missed the class, and she called me right back. She explained to me that she had two kids that had been on the same medication, and there were no problems. You also said that if I didn't the risk of having a pre-mature baby with lots of problems dramatically increases without the medication."

"Wow, didn't know that."

"Dad, you'd be surprised how many women take this medication during their later pregnancy. Several women at work told me about it, and a couple of my friends who have kids said they were on it too."

"Well you know, I told you that my administrative assistant was on it as well for her kids."

"So I just decided to take it."

"Good. What did you guys have for supper? Did your mother fix a big meal?"

"Nope. Domino's"

"Ah, you're mother was in heaven I bet."

"Yeah, she was. Afterwards, she made some chicken stuff that we're having tomorrow night."

"Sounds like the same stuff we had last night."

"Well, she's back downstairs, so do you want to talk with her?"

"No, tell her I'll call sometime this weekend."

"Are you serious?" Elizabeth asked.

"No, I am not serious. If she's available, put her on the line."

I talked with Linda for a few minutes and she relayed pretty much the same things that Elizabeth and I talked about. She told me that the shower was at 2 pm tomorrow and that she would call me in the morning before they left.

I closed my cell phone and sat back in the chair. The house was eerily quiet, and suddenly I felt very alone. It's odd in that when I travel to Kansas City and stay in the apartment for the week, I know it's just for a few days, so it's really not a big deal. Now though, I'm sitting in my own house and it's empty. Not sure I like this.

So, I turned on my brand new forty-six inch LCD television and put on the NFL network and settled back to watch Super Bowls from years past. Football will keep me company for the evening, and I watched it in the dark even though Elizabeth would greatly disapprove.

Later on the next evening, Linda called and gave me the download of the baby shower happenings. Being a male of the species, it's not part of my role to be in attendance at any type of shower, baby or otherwise. I rely on my wife to provide me with the goings-on from the inner sanctum of women's sacred rituals.

I did get pretty close once to being part of a shower. A couple of years ago, my mother threw Elizabeth a bridal shower. I was there to help set up the room, move furniture, and be a guest greeter at the door at my mother's request. After all the ladies arrived, I was to head back to my mother's house and pick up Jim and my brother, and we were going to go do manly things for a couple of hours. I have to admit, when I left the shower, there was a roomful of women all trying to talk at the same time. Sort of like that morning television show with the four women called *The View*. They were all talking at the same time and no one knew what the other was saying.

Anyway, it sounded like Elizabeth made quite a haul at her shower. It was put on by one of the women that was in Elizabeth's wedding, and who also happens to be pregnant. Many of the items that were on her list made it to the shower, so she was happy.

In the middle of our conversation, Linda asked me to hold on, and the next voice I heard was Elizabeth's.

"Dad," she said sounding very sleepy, "I just wanted to thank you for all the gifts that you and Mom have gotten us. I really appreciate it."

"That's ok, munchkin. I've taken care of you for all these years, so now I guess I'll move on to the next generation."

"Ok, I'm going to bed now. Love you."

And with that, Linda's voice came back on.

"She was very appreciative today. I wish you could have been here to see it."

"Yeah, I know. I wish I was there too."

Sunday of the same weekend I was sitting in the airport waiting for my morning flight, so I called Linda to check in and see what they were doing. I didn't even try calling on Linda's cell phone. I called directly on Elizabeth's phone and Linda picked up.

"Oh my honey, you should see this," she said. "Jim is upstairs trying to put the crib together."

"Where's Elizabeth?" I asked.

"That's what's so funny. She just went upstairs to check and see if Jim is putting the crib together right."

"Wow, that would be something to see."

"They're doing a good job."

I heard someone yell Hey! in the background on the phone, and I answered, "What?"

"Oh, that was just your daughter. She's just come downstairs with the camera and wanted to take a picture of her new rocking chair, but guess who's sitting in it?"

"You?"

"No. It's Chloe. She's already come to like the rocker a lot in the short time it's been here."

Ah, Chloe, the cat from hell. Haven't heard her name mentioned for a while. Looks like she's been staying in the background until the time is just right.

"So, I never asked you yesterday. Does Elizabeth look bigger than when you and I saw her at Christmas? I mean, is there a big difference?"

"Oh yeah," Linda replied. "When I walked in and saw her, I asked if she had put a basketball under her shirt."

I tried to get a mental picture of it. My mind flashed back to my days in high school during one of the pep rallies in the gym for the football team. Some of the cheerleaders had put on a skit, and I remember one of them walking out with a basketball under her cheerleader top. That was about as close as I could get to a picture in my mind.

"Have her take a picture and send it to me. I'd like to see."

"I took a bunch of pictures at the shower yesterday. It would probably be easier to look at those when you get back."

"Ok, they're calling my plane, so I'll call when I get in."

And with that, I closed my phone and boarded a plane that took me even further away from my home and family.

Over the course of that week, I finally got the scoop from Linda that she and Elizabeth have differing views of what cleanliness and organization of the house means to each of them. My wife is a very organized person who likes the house to be clean, neat, and orderly. When we first got married, that was so unusual to me. In college, I lived in an apartment with three other guys, and if you listen to Linda, it bordered on the edge of the movie *Animal House.* Yes, we had lots of parties (even a toga party), and consumed our fair share of adult beverages, and people were in and out at all hours of the day and night. Linda still talks about the time that dishes were piled in the sink for so long that there was a green mold growing on them. From my perspective, it was a *really* good time.

Then I went in the service and quickly got schooled on doing things the military way, so to have a woman clean the house and keep things running smoothly was completely foreign to me. I tried to help with the cleaning around the house, but Linda would always follow up behind me and redo it. After several times of this happening, I just slowly stopped cleaning. I mean why do it twice? I think Linda was relieved because she could now do it the Linda way. After twenty-eight years of marriage, I'm not sure I could go back to the old ways.

As usual, Linda dug in and started cleaning Elizabeth's and Jim's house from top to bottom the day after the baby shower. She's really good at it, and after years of trial and error, has really gotten it down to a science. She has these little gadgets for cleaning those little, dirty crevices, and for those hard to reach places. Since Elizabeth has been on bed rest, Jim has been doing the house cleaning. He's a good guy, but I'm sure he's been doing it in the typical guy way of cleaning which translates into not good enough. Both are good housekeepers, but not to the degree of Linda.

"Your daughter and I had a little discussion today on organization," she started.

"Oh yeah? I'm sure you showed her the Linda way of cleaning," I replied.

"I think she's a lost cause on that. I've been trying for years."

"Why? What was so bad?"

"Remember how the top of her dresser looked when she was in high school and college?"

A quick mental image crossed my mind of bottles and bottles of perfumes of different sizes, shapes, and colors; scads of nail polishes of every hue under the sun; various brushes and combs with hair entangled in the teeth; glittering necklaces twisted together; and other assorted trinkets layered upon the top of the dresser to the point where it was covered completely. It was the subject of many spirited discussions between my wife and daughter on cleaning day in our house.

"Yes, I do."

"Well, it's the same thing. All of her stuff piled on top to the point where you couldn't even see the doily that was on the dresser. I told her that it was fire hazard."

"Is that the only thing you two discussed?"

Somehow I knew it wasn't.

"Oh no. We also talked about her closet and the shoes and boots thrown all over the place."

"Was it like in her apartment?"

Elizabeth lived by herself in an apartment for about two years after she graduated from college. The times Linda and I would visit were always an impending surprise of how the apartment would look on our arrival. Her closet was an overwhelming intertwined mass of clothes, both clean and dirty, hanging in various states of disorder. On the floor were piled an amazing amount of shoes and boots scattered everywhere. I'm not sure how she ever found matching pairs of shoes to wear.

"Probably worse I think," she answered.

"She's just like you. Shoes, shoes, shoes."

"No, no. I may have a lot of shoes, but they are all in their boxes in the closet neatly stacked and arranged alphabetically by color."

See what I mean?

"I know. She's just not like you when it comes to organization," I said consoling.

I heard a sigh on the other end.

"Hopefully things will get better once she sees that she has to be organized for the baby," I said.

"Yeah, maybe, but I'm not holding my breath. You know the worse thing?"

Here it comes.

"I was making their bed, you know, changing the sheets, and all that. I pulled up the mattress to do my hospital fold, and I found one of her slippers wedged between the mattress and the wooden support. I pulled it out and looked around for the other one. I couldn't find it, so I tossed it on the floor and finished making the bed. I was dusting the floor with a dry mop and got down to look under the bed, and guess what I found?"

"Things you didn't want to see?"

"Well, yeah, but also the other slipper. I tried to get it, but I couldn't reach that far. So I just threw the other slipper under the bed with it. Now she has a matched pair."

"Really?"

"Yeah," she said laughing. "It will give her something to work for."

The following week, Linda's cell phone rang early one morning. It was Elizabeth.

"Hey, why didn't someone let me know that Ryan was coming?"

"Well, I think your mother was supposed to tell you, but it looks like she didn't."

"It's no big deal since he's not staying here, but I didn't have the bed made up or anything. Actually I was upstairs in bed reading with a towel wrapped around my wet hair.

"It's ok. It all worked out, right?"

"Yeah I guess."

"So do you want to talk with your mother?"

"Yeah, that's fine," she said sullenly.

Jeez. Somebody got up on the wrong side of the bed.

§ Chapter 7

People I Wished You Could Have Met

One of the things that is sad to me is that you'll never experience the love and adoration from some of the people who truly loved me and your grandmother as we were growing up. I want to tell you about them so you'll understand where you come from.

My father, your great-grandfather, was one of five boys who grew up in a very small village, just a cross-roads really, of houses named Greenfield, about two miles from where I grew up. He was the youngest of the boys and had two younger sisters. He was solidly built and had a barrel of a chest. He had been a weightlifter in his younger years, and had a brown belt in judo. He was not someone that you messed with unless you were serious, and then only at your own risk.

One thing I learned about my father was that he was tough as nails as a kid. There's a story that one of his brothers, Uncle Edward, told me that shows just how tough he was. When he was only six or seven, I guess there was a bigger kid who wanted my father to steal something for him. My father refused, so the bigger kid started to twist his arm to make him do it. My father still refused, and the bigger kid kept twisting his arm and ended up breaking my father's arm before his brothers finally figured out where he was and took care of the older kid, if you know what I mean. I guess my father didn't flinch during that whole time.

He was a very good man, but when he was younger, he was prone to being a smart guy. What do I mean by that? He quit high school in his senior year and joined the Marine Corps. Quit his senior year. He had six months to go and he would have graduated, but as he told the story, you couldn't tell him anything back then. He was very stubborn. He then enlisted in the Marine Corps and ended up going straight to Korea right after boot camp. He was there for over a year, and ended up getting wounded while he was there. When he returned, he met my mother and they ended up getting married, and built a house just a hundred yards or so from where my mother grew up.

He was the type of man that liked the simple things in life. He loved his family dearly and would do anything for them; he loved my mother, your great-grandmother, dearly as well; he liked to hunt and fish; he coached football and baseball; he loved the Steelers, although at times it was hard to tell depending on how they were playing; he never missed a day of work in his life, and you could set your watch every morning with the time he left for work.

One very little known story is that he tried out for a major league baseball team, the Detroit Tigers, as a pitcher. He was a very good baseball player, and excelled at pitching. He and a cousin went to Detroit for a tryout to see if they could make it in the major leagues. Well, I guess it's not too hard to tell that he didn't get picked up by the Tigers. He would laugh and say that they told him don't call us, we'll call you.

He worked in a steel mill most of his adult life, until just before he retired, when he drove a truck for a local window and door company for a couple of years. He worked very hard in the mill, and I always remember him coming home and falling asleep in his chair watching television. Oh, he loved his movies. He is the one that taught me to love the great actors when they made movies that were really movies. I grew up watching John Wayne, Audie Murphy, Clark Gable, Gary Cooper, and all the action stars of westerns and war movies. No matter how many times we watched them, whenever they came on the television, we watched them again and again.

Unfortunately, he was taken too soon from us. He went into the hospital for triple bypass heart surgery and never came out. He came through the surgery fine, but several days later, a blood clot broke loose and caused a stroke. He was life-flighted by helicopter to a hospital in Pittsburgh where they tried to help revive him with a new experimental drug to dissolve the clot, but they were too late. He had been retired for just two months. He actually stayed on the job a extra few months so he could train his replacement. It was such a shock to everyone.

The day of the funeral, there were people lined up all the way around the funeral home for hours so they could pay their last respects. The funeral director said that it had been a long time since he had seen so many people attend a funeral.

It was one of those mid-September days when the sun would shine for a brief time, and then it would cloud up and rain very hard. We drove to the small cemetery in a motorcade, and the casket was brought out and put under a tent, with the American flag draped over it. I remember it was raining and cold during that time. I looked up to heaven and asked God to please give us a break. You took him from us, now please let us bury him with some respect. It was at that point that the old bugler from the VFW Honor Guard began playing taps, and the clouds suddenly opened up and revealed spectacular sunshine. I will always remember that.

There were many things that my father taught me like how to defend myself; how to throw a curve ball; and how to watch the ball carrier's hips when you want to make a tackle; and he guaranteed that each of his kids would graduate from college. Yes, those were all important, but the most important thing I learned from him was how to stand up for myself when I thought I was right. I have carried that with me all my life. I have tried to teach that to your mother, and I think you'll find out that I succeeded.

There are so many things that I want to tell you about him. He would have treated you like a princess or prince. He would have just loved you to pieces. You should have seen how his eyes lit up whenever your mother and Uncle Ryan would come to visit when they were just kids. He would go out and do things in the yard with them like letting them drive the yard tractor, much to my mother's dismay, and just generally enjoyed them. He was considered a Korean War hero, and his name is inscribed on a monument along with all the other brave men from the community, just a few miles from where he is buried.

Your great-grandmother grew up just a few hundred yards from where she raised her family in Bethel. She and her brother, great-great Uncle Don, lived in the small house just down the road from where she grew up, and it was right next to the school house. Back then, all the kids went to a local one room school where one teacher usually taught students from first through eighth grade. She started out there and then, but a new school was built in the nearby town, and all the kids had to ride the bus to go there. It was new experience for all them.

When she was in high school, she was a cheerleader and part of the homecoming queen court in either her junior or senior year. A year or so after she graduated, she met your great-grandfather and got married. About eleven months later, I was born, and the family was started. For their first year of marriage, they lived in a small apartment in the same little cross-roads town where your great-grandfather grew up. Actually it was right around the corner. They then built the house near where she grew up and stayed there for the rest of their lives.

If there was ever a matriarch of a family, your great-grandmother certainly took on that role. I say that as a great compliment to her. She was the one that ram-rodded everything. She knew when and where everyone had to be and made sure that they got there. She got us up at a specific time in the morning and we all knew had a exact amount of time in the bathroom before the next kid was scheduled. I remember that she would plan meals around sports, whether it was on television, or if one of us had an actual game. Whenever we got home late from practice, there was always something left warming for us in the electric skillet.

She was the one that actually pushed me to go to college, although your great-grandfather's threats of bodily harm helped convince as well. She filled out all the paperwork and financial documents and sent them off for me. I always knew that I would go to college, but it was one of those situations where 'I'll do the paperwork later.' If it hadn't been for her pushing, I'm not so sure I would have made it to school in that first semester. I remember her telling me one time that my father told her that if he hadn't met her, he probably would be living in a small, dungy apartment near the steel mill and never made anything of himself. That was a great compliment to her.

She was very smart, and should have gone onto college, but she never had the opportunity when she was younger. She didn't work when we were kids, but later on as we grew older, she got a job at the high school as the principal's secretary. She was very

113

good at her job, always organized and knew what was going on. Everyone knew who ran the office, and it certainly wasn't the principal.

Instead of taking the bus each morning, I would ride with her to the school. It was sort of a treat. It was fun to get in before all the other students when the halls were empty and quiet. I would usually hang out in the cafeteria with one of the football coaches, who sold student lunch tickets in the morning before school, and we would talk. The school buses would arrive one after another and the hallways would come alive with noise and voices. As I got older, I still rode with her to school, but the cafeteria got a little old after a while, so we would hang out down where the cool kids were.

I would actually go out a few minutes early each morning and sit and warm up the car for us. It was so cool to be thirteen years old and sitting behind the wheel of a big Ford car letting it get warm. I actually learned to do most of my driving during those trips to and from school. When I first got my learner's permit, she would let me drive in the morning to school. It really wasn't that difficult because it was four miles of straight road, and we had to make one left turn to get to the school. Sometimes she would take me out to drive on the way home from school and we would go on winding roads so I could learn how to maneuver the car and keep it in my lane. We never had any close calls, and it was a lot of fun. I'm not so sure she would have said it was, at least not in the beginning.

She was always so proud of her family, and worked tirelessly to make sure we had everything that we needed. She never missed a game that any of us played in no matter how far away it was. She taught most of us to drive, and pushed all of us to college. She would sit and review our school work with us if we were having trouble. She was the first person that we told problems to, no matter the subject. She was also the first one to tell us when we weren't doing our best, and sometimes in a not so subtle way.

There was one time when I was fifteen years old, and I was pitching in a baseball game. Your great-grandfather didn't make it to the game because of work, but your great-grandmother was there. I was not having a very good game, and the coach finally pulled me out about mid-way through the game. I was so frustrated and upset with my performance, I cursed and threw my glove from the pitcher's mound all the way across the field to our team's bench. Well, she would not have any of that. She made her way onto the field and grabbed me by the arm and pulled me off the field all the while scolding me for cursing and throwing my glove. I learned a good lesson that day.

She would also do whatever she had to do to protect her family. I was playing in a softball game against a rival, and the score was close and the game was getting heated. One of the other team's players hit a long drive down the third base line and it looked like it was going to be a homerun since there was no fence. Your great-uncle Bob happened to be the umpire on the third base line. He was probably sixteen at the time, and had never been an umpire before. He had just come to watch, and they had pulled him out of the stands to do it. Well, as the player was in a full sprint rounding second base to run to third, great-uncle Bob called it a foul ball. The player couldn't believe it. He became very angry and sprinted over to where great-uncle Bob was standing and started screaming at him face to face. Well, that's all your great-grandfather needed to see was someone intimidating one of his boys. I could see the veins pop out on his neck which was a bad sign. It usually meant someone was going to get thumped. He jumped out of his chair, and was going to head over to the altercation, but your great-grandmother grabbed him by his belt before he could get very far, and dragged him back to his chair and sat on his lap. All he could do was yell at that point. Luckily, cooler heads prevailed quickly, and disaster was averted. To this day, I don't think that guy knows how close he came to ending up in the hospital courtesy of my father. He has my mother to thank for that.

The final person that I want to tell you about from my side of the family is my grandmother, Sarah, which would be your great-great grandmother. She was born in 1909, in Farrell, PA, a small mill town known for the thriving ethnic diversity of Italians, Poles, Swedes, English, and Slovaks. She was the youngest girl of seven children, with one brother younger than she. Her father, who came to America from England when he was twenty-one, landed and settled there because of the job opportunities at the steel mills.

I don't know much about her childhood, other than the stories I remember her telling us about people like the iceman with his horse and wagon, and following him and chewing on the chips of ice that fell. She told us about how strong the iceman seemed when he would load up a big block of ice onto his shoulder and climbed the stairs from the street to the house. Where the family lived, the town is actually a series of very steep hills. Once you navigated the hills on the streets, there were long cement stairs that rose to the rows of houses perched at the top. I remember going to visit relatives and climbing all those stairs as a kid. The houses always seemed so far away, almost in the clouds.

She eventually got married to my grandfather, Elmer, and moved from town to a small house in the country. He also worked in a steel mill in Farrell. They had two children, my mother, Judy, and my uncle, Don. As I said before, they lived next door to the school, so I'm not sure they had any days off due to snow.

My grandfather died when I was three or four. After he passed away, she moved into my mother and father's house with the rest of the family. She lived there for several years, and then got remarried to a man by the name of Orville. He owned a small house nearby and she moved in there.

It was a small, pale green house that sat on a knoll in the middle of big, grassy lot. On one side was a horse pasture that was fenced in, and on the other side was an older couple with a tan brick house. I have a memory of staying overnight at their house when I was very young. Orville loved to watch professional wrestling, known as studio wrestling then, and after supper, he and I sat there that night in the dark and watched the show televised live from Pittsburgh. I remember getting scared at one point because one of the wrestlers, Killer Kawalski, a large bald man dressed in a black leotard, grabbed the microphone from the interviewer and started chewing on it while staring into the camera. He looked so mean and ferocious to a five year old.

It's interesting what you remember about people as a kid. I remember Orville's hands always seemed to be shaking a little, only to find out as I grew older, that he had the beginnings of Parkinson's disease. He would sit in a chair in the small kitchen at their house and my grandmother would put shaving cream on his face, and then slowly shave him. His hands shook too much for him to do it for himself. He had brilliant white hair, what was left of it, and also had an eyelid that didn't completely open. He always tilted his head back to look at you. He also liked the small bulldog-looking breed that seemed to sniff and snort at you whenever you got close to them. Friendly, just lots of slobber.

Probably the biggest thing I remember about him was that he disliked kids, and there were four of us who were loud and rambunctious for him to dislike. Many times we as a family would go to their house to visit and Dad and the kids would stay in the car. Mom would go in and visit for a while, and Dad had to entertain us in the car.

Your great-great grandmother Sarah was a quiet, thoughtful, and artsy woman. One of the things that was stacked against her was narcolepsy all of her life. When she was young, it was not recognized as a disease, and she was labeled as stupid and slow. I think those tough times shaped her for the rest of her life. She would sit on the couch or a chair reading the paper or watching television, and she would fall asleep within minutes. Many times she would complain that she sat down to watch her favorite tv program only to sleep through the whole thing. She never learned to drive because she was afraid she would fall asleep at the wheel.

She was so creative when it came to arts and crafts. One of her past times was to dry out flowers from her flowerbeds, pansies were her favorite, and arrange and frame them to use as decoration. She was a wonderful artist, and you would find little sketches of people's faces on newspapers, scrap paper, or napkins around the house. She was the person who showed me how to draw a face, and I would look through her art books that taught the finer points of drawing humans. Luckily your mother has inherited her art gene.

You could always tell when a baby was due by someone in the family because she would crochet booties for them. There was always yarn and crochet needles lying around the house. Later on in life, she took up quilting and would meet with a group of women weekly at the church, and they would spend the day together making gorgeous quilts that they sold to benefit the church.

She was a coin collector and each child, upon their birth, received a full set of pristine coins for the year that they were born. I still have mine. She couldn't walk through the yard at the house without finding a four-leaf clover. She was magical at that. She had a beautiful voice and you could hear her always humming or singing as she crocheted, or cleaned or whatever she was doing at the time.

She went through a period of making small, wrinkled people using crabapples. She would use a ripe crabapple, and pinch it into a face, and then let it sit at room temperature for several days. During that time, she would construct a small body out of pipe cleaners, and sew together small dresses or pants and coats to put over the pipe cleaner body. After that, she attached the apple head, which by now, was brown and wrinkled, and placed them in a small chair she had cut out using a milk carton. It was one of the more creative things that she did with her skills.

She lived to be a ripe old age of eighty-nine. Unfortunately, she had the onset of dementia at that point and really didn't know anyone. I remember getting a call from my mother late one evening that she had gone into the hospital from the nursing home. I was up and getting ready early the next day to make the five hour trip back home when my mother called to tell me she had passed away that night of a stroke.

I was stunned. She was the first person that I loved who died while I was an adult. Several other close relatives had died when I was very young, and I have no actual memory of the funeral.

It was an emotional time for me. I remember walking into the funeral home the first time and breaking down into tears when I looked at her lying in the coffin.

It has been over twelve years since then, and time has a way of healing all wounds. I do visit her gravesite from time to time when I am back home. She is buried in the family plot on a hillside overlooking a small valley. She is home with those she loves.

* * *

Your great-grandfather on your mother's side was born in Italy, and made the trip to America when he was just one or two years old. One of the funny things is that all of his birth records were lost, so no one really knew how old he actually was. He had "an about" age that we always celebrated. Plus he didn't really know what, or if, he had a middle name, and what it was. He adopted the letter 'J' as his middle name, but it didn't really stand for anything. He was the youngest boy of seven children. His mother died when he was young, so his older sister, Peppie, raised him and the two younger sisters.

He was a very good athlete in high school and lettered in football, baseball, and basketball in very small town. He was given a scholarship to play football and attend Edinboro University, but back then it was known as Edinboro Teacher's College.

After college, the Second World War broke out and he enlisted in the Navy. He served the entire war at a base in Florida. Even though he never left the States, he served his country well.

After he got out of the Navy, he headed back to his roots in Pennsylvania and ended up in a small town called Sheffield. He started out there as a teacher and football coach. There were many old pictures of him in his younger years with his teams. I remember him telling stories about this player or that player like it was yesterday only to find out that it happened forty-five years ago. He also coached basketball at Sheffield and actually had a couple of undefeated seasons in both football and basketball. He also coached the only college All-American from that school who went on to play football at the Naval Academy. That same man, Steve Eisenhower, is also a member of the college football Hall of Fame.

During that time, he met your great-grandmother, Theresa, and started a family as well. You know that because you wouldn't be here with out it.

Later on, he became principal of the high school and the legend was written. He was the high school principal for well over twenty-five years, and was considered one of the few very good administrators in the school district, or maybe the state, depending on who you talk with. He did get his master's degree from Slippery Rock State College, now known as Slippery Rock University.

He was always lending a hand to those less fortunate, especially those kids of Italian descent. He was considered a pillar of the community. When he was a coach, he would invite the football team over for spaghetti the night before the game. He and Theresa would host twenty high school boys in their small apartment and feed them until they couldn't eat any more. The sauce was homemade, as were the meatballs, along with fresh, homemade bread. He always said that was the reason that they played so well.

He was very old-fashioned. He always ate homemade bread, sauces, and the like. He use to tell a story about a marital moment he and your great-grandmother had just after they were married. It seems he came home from work one day with a twenty pound bag of flour, and put it on the kitchen table. Your great-grandmother asked him what that was for. He proceeded to tell her that she was to start making homemade bread. She looked at him and said that she never had made bread before. He said that he knew that, and that's why he got such a big package of flour so when she was done screwing up all the bread from this bag, he would go get her another one.

Somewhere during that time, they moved from the small apartment to a large house. Their family started to grow once they moved in. It would probably be a good time to bring up that your grandmother is adopted. She was about six months old when she was adopted by your great-grand parents. Although she was light-haired and fair-skinned, they always explained it that she was from southern Italy.

Your great-grandfather was an avid gardener. Most of the yard at the house was taken up by his garden, and every year it seemed to get bigger until your great-grandmother put a stop to the growth. His produce was well-known in the community, and he was actually famous for his tomatoes, garlic, and zucchini. After he retired, he would get up at four in the morning and go walking with one of his buddies. They'd make it back to the house around seven, and have coffee and oatmeal. After that, he would go out into the garden and hoe or pick weeds, or do whatever needed done. He usually only wore a pair of shorts and garden shoes. His shorts always hung way down since he had a big belly. Your great-grandmother would scold him about putting on a shirt when he was in the garden, but he never did. And he would get so tan. He was olive-skinned to start with, so any type of sun would just deepen the color.

He had rows and rows of books about every conceivable plant you could grow in a garden in northern Pennsylvania. He would get his seed books in the mail in January and make his selections of what he wanted to plant that year. His seeds would show up in March, and he would start them in these little planters. The entire back porch would be filled from the floor to the ceiling with little plants waiting to be transplanted from their small perch in the porch to the tilled and fertilized soil of the back yard. I think these were actually his kids, sort of like when he was the principal in school.

He also liked to brew his own beer and wine. I can't vouch for the beer, but I did see vats of wine being slowly fermented from grape juice into wines of all different flavors. He and one of his buddies would make a trip to Erie, PA every summer and buy different grape juices. He would bring them back along with several of the large, plastic bottles from the tops of water fountains. These were his vats to make his wine. He would do all the calculations for the yeast and sugar, and then put the contraptions together so the wine could "breathe". At the end of the fall, he would bottle the wine and give it away as Christmas gifts. It got to the point where he had his own labels made, and concocted several types of wine that were considered quite good by his family, as well as quite strong.

He did like his martinis. He and your great-grandmother would stop whatever they were doing at five pm each day and have a martini and a few crackers or chips. I remember one time he and I were working on a project for the garden when your grandmother and I visited one summer. We were getting all the tools out, and I asked him how long he thought it would take for us to get the job completed. He looked up at the garden, scratched his chin, and looked back at me, and said, "Probably three martinis."

There were probably two highlights of his life as a coach that he was very proud of. The first was when he was inducted into the Pennsylvania Football Coaches Hall of Fame in Hershey. Everyone came down from Sheffield to witness the historic event. Your grandmother, mother, Uncle Ryan, and I were already living in Carlisle, so it was just a short drive to Hershey for us. It was such a great time. His former student, and All-American running back, made the induction speech and presented him to the large gathering in the auditorium. The inductees before him were quite emotional in their speeches, but he wanted to liven things up. He threaded several jokes into his acceptance speech and he had the crowd in the palm of his hand.

The second was when they renamed the high school gymnasium after him. I think I was actually in the service when that happened, so I don't remember it. I can tell you that there is a gleaming metal plate at the entrance to the gym with his name on it.

It was just three years ago this month that he passed away. He had gotten a really bad cold which turned into pneumonia and it just got worse. He didn't like hospitals, so he waited until the very last moment to go in, and by then, it was too late. We had gotten a call from a relative that he was going into the hospital, and your grandmother made the trip from our home near Pittsburgh by herself. I couldn't go with her right then because of my work. Your grandmother stayed overnight with him in the hospital. I worked the next day, which was a Thursday, and then drove up unannounced to the hospital to be with her. We stayed together with him on Friday, and I went back to the house for some sleep later that evening. I got a call around 3 am that he had passed away, so I made a quick trip into the hospital to be with your grandmother.

Much like my father's funeral and service, there were people standing in line for hours to see him for the last time. Prior students, friends, former athletes that played for him, former coaches, and administrators all filed past him to pay their last respects, some being pushed in wheelchairs, or walking slowly with canes. There were many stories of sports, or fishing, or conversations that were told that evening. It was a great tribute to him.

Lastly, your great-grandmother on your mother's side, Theresa, was born in the small town in the mountains of PA, just a few miles from where she finally ended up living in Sheffield. She was the oldest girl of four children in her family. Her father worked at the gas company, and eventually they moved to Sheffield.

She was somewhat of an independent woman in her time. After she graduated from high school, she entered into nursing school and left for California. Actually, there is a side story here. Her mother and youngest brother, Larry, went to visit her during that time. Larry was twelve or thirteen at the time, but he has vivid memories of the visit. He liked it so much that he moved from Pennsylvania to near San Francisco and has lived there most of his adult life.

She stayed in California for quite a while, mostly going to school and then worked as a nurse during the Second World War. She returned back to Sheffield, worked as a nurse in the local hospital, and ended up meeting your great-grandfather. She told a funny story about their first date. He called her one evening, and not known for his gift of gab or pleasantries, quickly asked her if she had time to get a sandwich and a beer with him. She said she did, and always said that she could never have turned down that type of an offer.

They settled finally on Church Street in Sheffield and

adopted your great uncle Tom, and your mother. She stayed at home while the kids were small. After they were old enough and in school, she went back to nurses training and worked in the hospital again, and off and on as the school nurse.

Now think about how your mother and great-uncle must have felt when they went to school. Their father was the principal, and their mother was the school nurse. No way they could have gotten away with anything with that deck stacked against them.

She was always quick to laugh either at a joke or herself. One of the funny things that happened is whenever she drank just a bit too much beer or wine, her nose would get bright red. We always laughed at that when it would happen.

She was very religious, as was most of her side of the family. In fact, she was often referred to as Mother Theresa, in honor of the nun who worked with the poor in India. She went to church most everyday, and was a member of numerous religious and civic organizations that provided charity and help to those in the community.

With a maiden name of Fitzgerald, her family was from Ireland. They followed some Irish customs like eating corned beef and cabbage on Saint Patrick's Day, and she had Irish flags and memorabilia all around the house. Not to be outdone, your great-grandfather did his part with Italian flags as well.

Her side of the family always had a huge reunion every year of the O'Leary family, the main Irish family of which all the others sprouted from. We attended several times, and the ball room would be completely filled with people from all over the country from the family. Your great-grandmother was always in charge of something, whether it was the room set-up, or rooms for people just to relax. They had great activities like matching peoples' faces with their family, and there was always a family tree that was updated with the newest members of the clan.

She was the consummate party host. All the large gatherings, whether it was for holidays, or festive occasions, were always held at their house, and she made sure everything was just right. It was nothing for her to get up at five in the morning and make five loaves of homemade bread for a party, or the meal that night. You have no idea just how wonderful the smell of homemade bread is when you wake up on a frosty morning. It was a standard for her every Saturday.

She was the organizer of the family. She kept meticulous records of everything. We found that out even more so after both had passed. She had written down every purchase with all the information and stored it in a small metal box. It was really incredible.

She passed away in 2002, actually the Saturday before Mother's Day in May. She had been having trouble with her health as she got older. She had lupus in her later years which made it joints stiff and sore. Your great grandfather had a hot tub installed in the house, and she soaked in it each day which relieved some of the pain, and allowed her for better movement. It got to the point that she couldn't get into the tub anymore, so it didn't add much help.

She had been having mini strokes, and it got to the point where they were happening quite frequently. Your grandmother made the trip to Sheffield on Mother's Day weekend to spend some time with her. Unfortunately she had a more severe stroke and they rushed her to the hospital. A few hours later, they learned that she had passed.

During the funeral in the church, there was not a dry eye in the place. She seemed to have touched most everyone in the community in one way or another. The church was filled with members of all the civic and charity groups she was a part of, and it was long motorcade to the cemetery.

I remember one thing that she said when she had gone through a series of mini strokes, and had been taken to the hospital. She said that as she laid there on the table, she had a talk with God, and that she was prepared for the next step.

Her deep religious convictions guided her in her life, the raising of her children, and had now reinforced her in the hour of need. There are no questions in my mind that she is looking down on us now.

§ Chapter 8

Eviction Notice

Elizabeth had been in real discomfort with a lot of pain in her back lately. There were very few positions where she felt comfortable. The best one was actually sitting in the edge of her big easy chair with two pillows behind her back. As for rest, I guess she was getting three to four hours of restless and painful sleep.

As usual, I was traveling.

"I just wanted to tell you that Elizabeth is at the hospital," Linda said during one of our nightly calls.

"What for?" I asked quickly.

"Oh, she said she found some blood, so she called the doctor and he said to come in."

"How much blood?"

"Not much because she's already on her way home. You know your daughter, she could find a pinhead spot and she's on the way to the emergency room."

"Well, yeah, but we're getting down to brass tacks now," I replied.

"She's fine," came Linda's reply.

A day later, Elizabeth called.

"Hey Dad, I just wanted to let you know about my latest doctor's appointment."

"Cool, what did he say?"

"Well, he said that the baby should be between eight and

125

nine pounds at the end of the nine months."

"Wow, that's pretty big, huh?"

"Dad, I about fell off the table when he told me that."

"Aren't you the one that said that nature fits the baby to the mother?"

"Yeah, but I think someone made a mistake this time."

"How far along are you?"

"He measured me and said I was thirty-six weeks."

"So you're ok if the baby comes early?" I asked.

"Yeah, so if the baby comes early, there shouldn't be any problems."

"Wait until I get home though, ok?"

"I'll do my best," she said with a laugh.

The next day, my phone rang and it was Linda.

"I just wanted to call and let you know that Elizabeth is at the hospital again."

"Really?" I asked looking at my calendar to see what I could rearrange if I had to leave.

"She's having some pain, and some pretty regular contractions, so the doctor said to come in."

"Do you think this is it?" I asked from 900 miles away.

"No, I don't think so. She's still a month away, so I think it's at least a week or two away."

"Ok, let me know if anything changes."

I made it back to Pittsburgh that Friday without any further problems, weather or otherwise. Saturday passed with no real issues. Elizabeth called just to complain.

I was in a deep sleep when the phone rang and shocked me awake. I heard Linda answer it as I looked at the clock through sleepy eyes. The numbers showed a blurry 1 am. Linda hung up the phone and lay back in bed.

"That was Jim. They're going to the hospital again. Elizabeth is having some strong contractions."

"Another false alarm?"

"I don't know. They'll call once they find out what they say."

I fell back to sleep only to be shocked awake again by the phone. It was 3 am. I heard Linda talking softly.

"Ok. Yeah. Call if anything changes." She hung up the phone and sat on the edge of the bed.

"They're admitting her this time."

"So I guess this is it?"

"It looks like it."

I rolled over. I've read that the first pregnancy labor is long, so I didn't have a panic to get in the car and race four hours across Pennsylvania at three in the morning. Linda lay back in bed, but just a few minutes later, she was up and moving around in the dark.

"What are you doing?"

"I can't sleep. I'm going to get up and start doing things around the house in case we have to leave quickly."

I watched the bedroom door open and close softly. I laid there for a while and must have fallen back to sleep. The next thing I knew, Linda was back in the bedroom.

"Are you going or staying or what?"

I looked at her sleepily. It was 6:15.

"What do you mean?"

"We have to get ready and go. I talked with Elizabeth again and she's in labor."

"Ok, we'll get packed and go."

"What are we doing with Ryan's car?"

Ryan had flown to Philadelphia that Friday to celebrate the impending wedding of one of his close friends with the group of guys he ran around with in high school. He left his car at our house and we were supposed to pick him up at five that evening. Nothing was ever easy.

I sat up in bed and rubbed the sleep from my eyes.

"We'll have to leave the car in the parking lot and hide the keys."

"How's he going to know where it is?" Linda asked. I could hear the stress level in her voice.

"I'll call him and tell him all that stuff."

"Ok, well come on."

Over the course of the next ninety minutes, the stress level inched up and up in the house. I tried to stay out of the way and help Linda with packing, and things like that, but mostly tried to stay out of the way. I filled a cooler of food to take with us since we had just gone to the grocery store the previous night and got a huge amount of food. I could hear Linda muttering that she should have left at 3:30.

127

When Ryan was born, we went through the same thing. Linda had been having fairly strong contractions for several days. I kiddingly told her that she'd have to wait until the Super Bowl was over (the next day) before we could go to the hospital. Funny, I didn't learn anything from the first time she was pregnant.

We made it through Sunday (Super Bowl), but Linda was in a lot of discomfort. Next thing I know, she's shaking me awake in the middle of the night that we need to go to the hospital. I trudged to the bathroom half-awake and started shaving. A few seconds later, she appeared in the doorway.

"We need to go. NOW!"

I quickly toweled off my half-shaven face, scooped up Elizabeth, and we ran for the car. On the way to the hospital, her water broke. It was a pretty wild ride. Luckily, nothing like that had happened to Elizabeth at this point.

Once everything was packed and in the car, (Side note: I had to take a couple of bags out of the car twice because I packed them too quickly.) I left a few minutes early to take Ryan's car to the airport. I parked the car, hid the keys, and walked over to the waiting area. A few minutes later, Linda came through with the car. I slid in behind the wheel and we headed down through the city to get onto the Pennsylvania turnpike and headed east towards Harrisburg.

A half hour into the trip, I asked Linda if she had heard from Elizabeth.

"Oh, I guess I didn't tell you. She called just after you left, and they were taking her in for a C-section."

A wave of panic slammed into my stomach.

"A C-section? Why?"

"She said that the baby was in distress, and the heartbeat wasn't where they wanted it, so they were wheeling her in."

Oh man, it's been many years since I've had this kind of quick stress, and having a just a few hours of sleep didn't make it much better.

"What else did she say?"

"That was it."

For the next couple of hours, we rode on, mostly in silence, broken only by a few conversations here and there. Linda was exhausted and napped for a few minutes at a time. We stopped about half way across the turnpike and got some breakfast and a much needed break. After filling up the car with gas, I eased back into traffic and continued our journey.

"You know," I started, "I've had all of these scenarios running through my mind, most of them terrifying." I wasn't sure if I should have brought it up.

"I know," said Linda. "I've had the same things going through my mind."

Ok, so I'm not the only one worrying.

We continued our journey through the sun-splashed day, both of us anxiously waiting for Linda's phone to ring with an update.

At about the three hour travel mark, Linda sat up in the seat.

"Should I call?"

"Yeah, call."

"What if they're in the middle of something?"

"Well, just text them," I suggested.

"What should I say?"

"Say something like 'any updates, question mark."

Linda typed in the message and hit the send button.

"Hopefully we'll get something back soon," she said softly as she sat back.

Minutes slowly went by, and then turned into an hour. Still no message or phone call. We rode on in silence.

Finally, her phone rang. Linda grabbed it and flipped it open.

"Hi, how are you?" she said into the phone. Her face exploded into a huge smile as she listened. She turned toward me with the phone still to her ear.

"She had a baby boy, born at 9:14 this morning. Oh wow, you had him just as we were getting on the road."

More listening.

"He weighed six pounds, eight ounces, and was nineteen inches long."

More listening.

"Who are you talking to?" I asked.

"It's Elizabeth."

"Oh, I thought you were talking with Jim. Let me talk to her."

Linda handed me the phone.

"Hi Elizabeth, how are you?"

"Hi Dad, I'm really tired."

"I bet. You've been up most of the night, and I bet you haven't gotten any real sleep the last couple of nights either."

"No, it's been a long couple of days."

"A baby boy, huh?"

"Yeah, did Mom tell you how much he weighed?"

"She did. Six pounds, eight ounces. That's really good for a baby born a month early."

"Yeah it is. I can't believe what it would have been like at full term."

"Ok, you get some rest, and we'll be there soon. We're only about half an hour away."

I closed the phone and handed it back to Linda, who at this point, was in full tears.

"Well Grandma, what do you think? We have a baby grandson."

"I know. It's just so unreal," she said wiping away the tears with a tissue.

"The stress level just dropped a lot in here after that phone call," I said with a laugh.

"Oh yeah," she replied, and sat back in the seat. I could see her relax.

"What's his name?"

"She said that we had to wait until we got there. It's our punishment for not being there when he was born."

I called my mother and informed her. She was ecstatic. She made sure that I knew I was to call all my siblings, not her. Ok, I could do that.

We arrived at the hospital in downtown Harrisburg, and ended up parking on the top floor of the parking garage. Even though it was a Sunday, the garage was full. We took the elevator down to the first floor, and entered the main doorway. We had never been to this hospital before, and approached the matronly volunteer sitting at the front desk.

"Where would the maternity ward be?" I asked.

"Go down this hallway and take the visitors' elevator to the ninth floor."

Another step closer.

We rode the elevator up and exited on the maternity ward

130

floor. We stepped off and looked around. In front of us were two large, wooden doors with "Maternity Ward" stenciled over them. I tried pulling on the door, but it didn't move. I learned a long time ago that if you pull and the door doesn't move, then try pushing it. Well, that logic didn't work, still no movement.

A voice shouted from behind me, "You have to use the phone on the wall and call into the nurse. I turned to see an older woman, completely bald I might add, sitting in a wheel chair next to the wall dressed in dark sweats.

"Thank you," I said back to her.

I picked up the white receiver and waited for a voice since there were no buttons to push, or dials to turn. A female voice answered and I told her that we were they to see our daughter. I heard a soft click and the door silently swung open.

We tentatively walked through opening and looked around. I finally found the directions for the room numbers posted on the wall, and we followed them down to Elizabeth's room. The door was closed, so Linda knocked gently and pushed the door open only to be met with blue cloth curtains pulled across the entrance. She pushed them aside and we went in.

I saw nothing else in the room but our daughter lying in the hospital bed. The first thing I noticed were the freckles on her face. They usually don't show much, but they were really out in force now. Her hair was combed back, and her face looked tired. The covers were pulled up around her, and she had an IV in her right arm.

I looked around the room and saw Jim and his parents against the far wall. We said hello and exchanged hugs and congratulatory remarks, and then I went over to Elizabeth.

"You look so beautiful," I said to her as I leaned over and kissed her forehead.

"Oh Dad, no I don't."

"Yes, you do."

"Where's the baby?" Linda asked.

"His blood sugar was a little low, so he's in the nursery until his count comes back up," replied Jim.

"Yeah, well they said that he is supposed to be in the room no later than four hours after being born, so he should be here soon. There's only fifteen minutes left," injected Elizabeth.

"So what's his name?" Linda asked.

"His name is Benjamin Michael," said Elizabeth. "We liked the name Benjamin, and Michael is Jim's middle name."

"You know Ryan's middle name is Michael too. We now have three males with the middle name of Michael in the family. When can we see him?" I asked.

"You can see him now. Jim can take you down. He watched him get his bath this morning," said Elizabeth.

"Yeah, I'll take you down. Let's go."

Linda and I followed Jim down the hallway towards a large glass enclosure. We circled the glass until we found our grandson. There, lying in a large clear, plastic tub on a cart was my grandson. He was wrapped up in a blanket, I think they call it swaddled, under what looked like a warming heater, but it wasn't on.

I gazed at that beautiful little boy. He was perfect. His head was perfectly round, not squished like the other babies that had traveled down the birth canal. His cheeks were so pudgy and pink. I searched for any family resemblance. There it was...he had my daughter's nose which is exactly like mine. He did resemble his dad overall.

Linda was in tears and I put my arm around her. She sniffed and wiped away the tears, and we just stood there and looked. Our grandson. It seemed so unreal.

One of the nurses came over to him and unwrapped his blanket. She had some medical devices in her hand. She poked his heel to for blood to do a sugar test, and Benjamin did not like that, and he let her know that by filling the room with noise.

I must admit I was a little uneasy myself. I know that it had to be done, but he's my grandson and you shouldn't hurt him. My stomach was doing some somersaults at this point. I figured it was the large container of iced tea I drank all the way across Pennsylvania. You know, all the ascorbic acid.

With the test complete, and his results good, the nurse wheeled him down to the room with us in tow. We opened the door and in he went. Elizabeth raised the bed.

"You know, this is the first time that I've really seen him or got to hold him."

"Really?" I said.

"Yeah, my face was behind a sheet during the C-section, and they brought him around for me to see him for just a few seconds."

"Well, it's time you got to know our son," said Jim.

The nurse slowly picked up the small package and gently laid him in my daughter's arms. The room went silent except for the sniffing of Linda wiping away the tears. I must admit it was a grand sight.

We spent the entire afternoon with the newest member of our family. I did hold him which was something I had not done for quite a while. Linda handed him to me and I sat back in the large chair that Jim had been using to sleep in while he stayed in the room.

"Geez Dad, you're holding him like a football. Sit back and let him rest against your side," said my daughter, the new mother.

"I am, I am," I replied back. "He's new, so I don't want to dent him."

"Ahh, you won't dent him," cracked my wife.

Jim's parents had been there since early in the morning, and we took turns being in the room. Evidently there was a rule that no more than two grandparents can be in the room at the same time.

At our appointed time, Linda and I made out way up to the eleventh floor to the cafeteria. It had been over five hours since I had last eaten a small, and tasteless, egg and cheese sandwich from one of the rest areas on the turnpike. I was getting shaky from the lack of food. All Linda had was a hot chocolate when we stopped on the turnpike, but she can go for days without food. I'm lucky to survive several hours.

Linda got a hot dog and I picked up some chicken and fries. We sat at a table near the back and just basked in the glow of happiness.

"Can you believe it?" I asked.

"No I can't."

"We've been waiting and preparing for this day for eight months, and now it's here."

"We need to call people, you know," stated my wife.

"Yeah, but after I finish this wonderful meal of chicken and fries. Actually for hospital food, it's not that bad," I said.

I called my mother and informed her of all the statistics and the name, then my two brothers, my sister, and my uncle. Everybody made sure that I knew that I was a grandfather. Linda called her brother, and he was the only one that had issue with Benjamin's name. He thought Benjamin should have been named after him.

Jim's parents made their way back up to the cafeteria, and Linda and I went back to the room to be with the kids. Jim had come up with his parents so he could get something to eat and have some down time.

The four of us just sat in the room and talked and watched Benjamin. Elizabeth was still a little woozy from the anesthesia, and wasn't moving much due to the incision. She wasn't feeling any pain which is just the way she wanted it.

A nurse came in and took Benjamin back to the nursery for another test of his blood sugar. He was gone only a few minutes when Jim walked in.

"Where's the baby?" he asked.

"A nurse came in and took him to the nursery for a blood test," replied Elizabeth.

"Did you check her badge to make sure she was a nurse?" he continued.

"No," she said as a look of panic spread across her face.

"You need to do that," said Jim. "Remember what they told us."

"I'm sure it was a nurse," said Linda.

"Just to be sure, I'll take a walk down to the nursery," I said as I left the room. I needed to move around anyway.

Even though I was fairly sure it was a nurse that took the baby, a small voice in the back of my head made me walk just a little faster down the long hallway to the glass enclosure.

When I reached the enclosure, it was completely full of newborns. Just a few hours ago, there was only Benjamin and maybe one or two more infants. I slowly walked around the enclosure and peered through the glass at each of the babies lying in their plastic containers. I was just about to complete the full circle around the outside of the room, my heart beating faster with each step, when I spied my grandson. A nurse was working with him, taking his blood and temperature. I stood there for the entire procedure. I was still mesmerized by that little bundle. After several minutes, she looked up at me and motioned to her wrist. I assumed she thought I was the father. I shook my head no, and said I was just the grandfather.

"Hey, grandpas are important too, ya know," came a voice from behind me.

I turned my head and saw a nurse sitting at a desk with a television monitoring the locked door into the maternity wing. I just smiled.

The nurse gently placed Benjamin in his cart and wheeled him out of the nursery and down the hallway. I dutifully followed behind.

She opened the door and pushed the valuable cart into the room and left.

"Holy cow, I thought he was gone. I was getting a little worried," said Elizabeth.

"You don't have to worry," explained Linda. "There's no way Benjamin would have made it out of this hospital without your father knowing. He would have had this place in lockdown in two minutes with a battalion of Marines ringing the whole building."

"Yeah, I guess you're right," said Elizabeth as she lifted him out of the cart. "Hey Dad, I think it's feeding time for the little guy."

"I was thinking. I guess Benjamin got an eviction notice early, huh?" I remarked.

"Yeah, I guess you could say that, a month early" answered Elizabeth, and waved her hand.

That was my cue to leave the room. Elizabeth was going to nurse the baby, and there are some things that a father shouldn't see. I walked out into the hallway and down towards the plate glass windows at the end. It was still a brilliant day with the evening shadows getting longer as the sun slowly sank into the west.

I leaned up against the wall and looked out over the city from the ninth floor of the hospital, and marveled at what the day had brought. Twenty-four hours earlier, I had been glad to get back home from traveling, and was looking forward to a relaxing weekend, and spending a few minutes with Ryan after his trip. Little did I know that twelve hours later, I would be crossing the state feeling like a vice had a grip around my chest because my daughter was going in for a C-section to have the baby. Wow, talk about some roller coaster moments.

Linda came out of the room and walked down the hallway towards me.

"Well Grandpa, are you ready to head back to the house for some rest?"

I put my arm around her. "Who you calling grandpa?"

* * *

The next day, we had explicit instructions from Elizabeth to be at the hospital by 1:30 pm. Evidently Jim had to leave and go by his work to sign insurance papers, and Elizabeth didn't want to be alone. I can't blame her, and we didn't want her to be alone either.

At 12:30 pm, Linda and I walked out of the house and got in the car for the forty minute trip to the hospital. She was carrying a large half-moon green cushion with her that looked like a very large neck cushion you see people wearing on planes.

"Why are you taking a neck cushion for Elizabeth? Is it to prop up her head when the bed is reclined?" I asked as we started down the road.

"This isn't a neck cushion. It's for breast-feeding. It's called a boppy."

"Oh," I replied and figured I should probably be quiet.

"She can put this on her lap, or around her waist and hold the baby on it while she nurses."

"Got it," I said.

We got to the room around 1:30 and everyone in the new family was there. I held the baby and Jim took some video of all of us. It was a very important thing for him to get a video camera and shoot movies of the baby. He was always impressed that we had movies of our kids as they were growing up, and we watched them from time to time and laugh at the antics on the films. His family didn't have a video camera when they were growing up, and he wanted to make sure that he did.

A few minutes later, he left to complete his errands. Just a few minutes after that, Benjamin decided he was hungry and so out into the hallway I went again. I was a little smarter this time...I took the newspaper with me. After what seemed an awful long time, I was allowed back into the room to see my grandson.

"So you thought this was a neck brace, huh Dad?" Elizabeth said with a laugh as she held up the cushion

"Yes I did," I replied somewhat indignant. "I thought it was a big one, but hey, what do I know."

"I must say though, you were so innocent when you asked

me about it," said Linda as she put her arm around me.

"I didn't know. I was just trying to stay involved, you know," I replied.

A student nurse came in and said she needed to check Elizabeth's incision. Elizabeth turned to me and waved bye, and out into the hallway I went. Actually that happened quite a few times that day. I think I spent more time in the hallway during the first ninety minutes than anywhere else. Someone always seemed to be coming in and either checking Elizabeth or Benjamin for something. No wonder people come out of the hospital sick, they don't get any rest.

After the final banishment for a feeding, Linda came out later and said it was time to go.

"The kids are getting more company in a little bit, so let's give them some down time before all that happens."

"Ok, let's go, but can I say bye to them?"

"Yeah, go ahead."

I gently pushed on the door and poked my head inside. I saw Benjamin lying on my daughter's naked chest covered by a blanket.

"Dad, close the door!"

"I am, I just wanted to say bye, and I'll see you tomorrow."

"Ok."

And with that, I eased back out and closed the door.

As I walked down the hallway with Linda, a thought came to my mind. Pregnancy and giving birth is all about women, as it should be. They're the ones who do all the work, and burden much of the responsibility. You'll get no argument from me on that. As a male, I've tried to help out the best way I know how in this situation, which seemed to be woefully inadequate at times. I tried to help by getting things for Elizabeth or Jim, or asking if they needed anything. It appeared to me that my help wasn't really needed. After being the man that everyone depended on for so many years, it seemed that I was relegated to second string. I kept telling myself that this was the natural course of things, and I tried to remember what my dad did in this situation, but I was coming up empty. I think at one point during the day, Linda read my mind and sent me on a few errands to keep me busy, and feel like I was a contributing member of the new family unit. I appreciated it.

I was up early the next morning and got my laptop running to check in for work. I had been working half days the whole week so I could spend time with the kids. Linda's phone rang and I picked it up.

"Hey Elizabeth, how are you?" I said into the receiver.

"Oh, good."

"So are you and my grandson coming home today?"

"I hope so. They just took him down for a jaundice test just to make sure. If he passes that, we're coming home."

"Well, good. Do you want to call us when they test is done so we can set up coming home?"

"Yeah, that's probably the best way to do it," she replied. "I'll be glad to get home."

"I bet," and we hung up.

About an hour later, the phone rang again and we were given the all clear to head up to the hospital. Elizabeth wanted everyone there when she and Benjamin were discharged. Another reason was that we had Elizabeth's clothes she was wearing home from the hospital. I called to Linda, who was upstairs, that we needed to leave soon.

"We can't leave yet. I'm not done cleaning."

"It will be here when you come back," I called back.

"Ohhh!" I heard come from upstairs and then footsteps pounding overhead to the bedroom we had been staying in.

A few minutes later, Linda came down the stairs and we were out the door. The day was bright and sunny, and comparatively warm for the end of February. It took us about thirty minutes to get to the hospital, and then up to the room. Jim's parents were already there, and most of the items Elizabeth had with her were already packed into a couple of bags sitting on the bed. She was sitting in the small rocking chair in the corner with a pillow across her middle. Jim was sitting in the other chair holding Benjamin who was tightly swaddled in a white blanket.

"Well, hey, are we ready?" I asked as we made our way into the room.

"Yep, as soon as I get dressed. Did you bring my clothes?" asked Elizabeth.

"Right here in the bag," answered Linda.

"Ok, bye guys," said Elizabeth as she looked at her father-in-law and me.

We walked out into the hallway and made small talk while the girls got Elizabeth ready for the trip home. A few minutes later, the door opened and we were allowed back in.

Benjamin was lying on the hospital bed, and Elizabeth was struggling to get him into a newborn outfit, and then a big, furry jumper kind of thing. She was not having much success, and I sensed she was getting frustrated.

"How much sleep do you guys get last night?"

"Not much," she replied. "Ohhh, I can't get this stupid thing closed."

"Here," said Linda, "let me see if I can help."

Between the two of them, they managed to get Benjamin into the outfit, and then stood back to admire their work. The next thing was to get him into the car seat all snug and safe. After a few minutes of working, and being unsuccessful, they determined that the furry thing was too big for the car seat at this point. Elizabeth took it off of him, and then placed Benjamin in the car seat and put a blanket around him. Success.

A student nurse came in and asked Elizabeth if she wanted to ride down to the car in a wheelchair. She looked at me, and I nodded my head yes. A wheelchair appeared in the doorway and Elizabeth tried to sit down in it. After wrestling for several minutes, the footpad on the left side would not lie flat.

"Look, I'm not riding in this thing," she said as she slowly stood up.

"Is there a requirement for new mothers to ride in the wheelchair when discharged?" asked Jim's mother.

"No, it's actually their option," the student nurse replied back.

"Then I'm walking," stated Elizabeth, and she slowly started down the hallway.

We fell in behind in a line carrying the various bags and items from the room. Jim had gone down earlier to bring around the car to the front of the hospital. Jim's dad had a camera and was trying to get people to pose for shots as we walked, but he was getting little cooperation at this point. Benjamin was the only one that didn't seem to care one way or the other.

We popped out the front door of the hospital amid a throng

of people. It must have been shift change time, or lunch time, or both because there was a steady stream of people going in and out of the door. Jim had pulled the car up to the very front of the building, and was patiently waiting.

"Dad, check the car seat base and make sure it's tight," said Elizabeth.

"I checked it, it's tight," interjected Jim.

"I want my dad to check it as well."

I climbed into the car and looked at the car seat base.

"Put your knee on it with all your weight, and then pull the strap," explained Elizabeth.

I placed my knee into the plastic base, put all my weight on it, and paused. I didn't hear any snaps or cracks. That was a good sign. I gripped the seat belt and pulled with all my strength. My grandson's safety and well-being depended on it. The belt moved a little. I pulled again and nothing happened. I declared it was tight and safe.

Jim took the car seat from Elizabeth and snapped it into the base, and then the new Mom and Dad got in as well, Elizabeth in the back seated next to Benjamin. Jim's dad continued to snap away with the camera. We stood there in a group and watched them drive away as we waved. You would have thought that we wouldn't see them again for weeks, not just thirty minutes.

I put my arm around Linda, and we walked towards the elevator to the parking garage. It certainly was a beautiful day

www.ingramcontent.com/pod-product-compliance
Lightning Source LLC
Chambersburg PA
CBHW071003040426
42443CB00007B/641